MY FATHER
OUR FATHER

Dear Major & Mrs. Worthy:

Please accept this book as a
small token of my appreciation
for all the kindness to me and
all the intercessory prayers on
behalf of my family and myself.
May it be of inspiration
as you go on with the Lord's
work.

Much love,

Marialena Iglesias

7/94

MY FATHER
OUR FATHER

New prayers for personal
and congregational use

Compiled and edited by

Colin Fairclough

UNITED KINGDOM TERRITORY
101 Queen Victoria Street, London EC4P 4EP

First published 1994

ISBN 0 85412 616 3

Lieut-Colonel Colin Fairclough

first became acquainted with The Salvation Army in 1955, while serving with the Royal Navy. He entered the Army's London training college in 1958, and his first year of service was spent there as a cadet-sergeant. Appointments in the north-east of England followed, during which time Colin married Sonia, who had first introduced him to The Salvation Army. The years 1964 to 1968 were spent on the island of St Helena in the South Atlantic Ocean, followed by a short term at Port Elizabeth Central Corps in South Africa. From 1970 to 1974, Colin was principal of the Army's school for officer training in the Philippines. Following this, in 1975, came an appointment to Salisbury Citadel Corps in the then Rhodesia (now Zimbabwe). After four-and-a-half years there, the next move was to Canterbury Temple Corps, in the United Kingdom. Transfer to the Family Tracing Service took place in 1983, and Colin became Director of the service in 1986. He was elected to membership of the Association of British Investigators in 1992. The Faircloughs have four children, of whom two daughters and a son work for The Salvation Army in England and the USA.

Typeset by THQ Communications Resource Department

Printed in Finland by WSOY

Contents

INTERCESSORY PRAYERS

PART II — PRAYERS FOR PUBLIC USE

SUNDAY WORSHIP AND MIDWEEK MEETINGS — Prayers

CHRISTIAN CEREMONIES

THE CHRISTIAN YEAR

OTHER SPECIAL OCCASIONS

THE CHRISTIAN LIFE

MESSAGE OF COMMENDATION FROM THE NATIONAL LITERARY SECRETARY AND EDITOR-IN-CHIEF, USA

Declared William Law, 'He who has learned to pray has learned the secret of a holy and happy life.' In a sense we are all beginners at prayer — there are no experts. This anthology of prayer, skillfully researched and arranged by Colin Fairclough, offers a valued aid to our devotional experience, helping us to focus our minds on God and articulate our own deep longings.

The author has gathered this selection from an international roster of Salvationist pray-ers. The prayers are arranged in helpful groupings covering a wide range of special needs and occasions. The user will find, among others, prayers for Sunday worship, the offering, business meetings, child dedication, marriage services, retirements, funerals, special days of the Christian year, spiritual renewal and general prayers.

I commend this volume for everyone who aspires to bring prayer into the everyday needs and business of life. That, of course, includes each one of us enrolled in the lifetime school of prayer.

Colonel Henry Gariepy

MESSAGE OF COMMENDATION FROM THE ARCHBISHOP OF CANTERBURY

Each generation needs to learn to pray afresh whilst retaining a firm hold on the unchanging nature of God. In commending this book I hope that through it many will discover fresh insights into the nature and character of our Lord in deepening their relationship with him.

Introduction

From its conception, this anthology was intended as a 'working tool' for those engaged in the practice of prayer — whether in the privacy of the home, or in public worship before a congregation.

It is evident that the practitioner of prayer should be guided by the tool, and not controlled by it. Someone else's written prayers can never be precisely mine, but they will often lend me a flow of thoughts and words which I can own when my spirit and mind are searching. In this sense, a prayer is 'mine' in the same way that a hymn or a poem might be. Although this collection is divided into two main sections, it requires but a little imagination for many of the 'we' prayers in the book to become 'I' prayers, for use in the private place; whilst most of the private prayers can be enlarged for public utterance, whether in a family group or with a worshipping congregation.

With few exceptions, the prayers presented here have been written especially for this anthology. Prayers have been avoided which often appear in other compilations, and which tend to be drawn from frequently-used historical texts. The prayers are of a length with which most people at prayer will hopefully feel comfortable. They have come mainly from writers in the United States of America, Canada and Australia, as well as from the United Kingdom.

I am most grateful to all who responded so readily when invited to make a contribution, and to those others who submitted unsolicited offerings. The gracious words of encouragement which accompanied the manuscripts were of the greatest inspiration, suggesting that written invocations — both for private and public use — are sought after, even by those whose tradition leans toward the use of extempore prayer.

May the Holy Spirit of God breathe life into all of these prayers, and confirm them as the true heart-language of those who offer them.

Colin Fairclough

December 1993

PART I

PRAYERS FOR PRIVATE USE

OUR RELATIONSHIP WITH GOD

Into the divine presence

1

Almighty God, I have come into your presence, and I call you God. I have called you Lord; I have called you Father. I have entrusted you so often with the important concerns of my life.

I am here in faith, but what if my faith is misplaced? What if you are not there? What will happen to my words? Where will they go? Will they be wasted words? Will all this be wasted time?

Here, Lord, is probably the hardest part of my prayer-time — offering up my thoughts; pouring out the feelings of my heart; expressing my joys, my hopes, my needs, my problems; speaking to you on behalf of so many other people. And yet . . . and yet . . . you may not even *be* there . . . you may not even exist.

Lord, I am here with my doubts, as well as with my faith. I have to believe that you are there to hear me. Please help my unbelief.

Adoration and thanksgiving

2

Lord, it is an incredible and awesome thing that you are here with me now: the One who holds the stars in their courses just as surely holds me.

You sent me into this world with a unique set of finger-prints. Just another token of your individual care!

I find myself responding with wonder at the infinite variety displayed in the world of nature around me. Every creature and plant with its own intricate life-cycle. Thank you for planning mine.

Father, thank you for your quickening voice within my being today; that seal upon the truth revealed as I read your word.

Even before I was born I was known to you! All my days are already recorded in your book. What a sense of security this gives me!

Above all, thank you for Jesus, who made the way open for me to come into your holy presence, without fear.

Through him, I am accepted as your child, eternally safe in your love.

3

You do not always speak, Lord,
When I pray.
To tell the truth,
It's sometimes good
That way.

I say my piece,
Expose my deepest need,
And for my trembling brother
Intercede.
Make my thanksgiving,
Praise you, and adore,
For after all, that's what
My praying's for.
Peace seeps into my soul then,
I'm serene,
I know you're there
And silence falls between.
Companionable silence,
Mystic stuff,
That wraps me in your presence.
It's enough.

4

Lord, your joy is my strength;
In awe, I sin not but commune with you.
In my heart great storms arise
But the enemy is stilled
As you make the storm a calm.

    'Be still', you say, 'and know';
    'Stand still', you say, 'and see'.

You show me your love and power today,
Not in the earthquake or fire, but in the still, small voice.

    You rule, O Lord, and save,
    You lead, O Lord, where waters are still.

You speak from Heaven
And I am calm.

5

Beloved, in whom my soul delights, I will not let you go;
You are wholly beautiful,
Without a blemish.

The winter is now past,
   The rain is over and gone,
      The flowers appear on the earth,
         And the time of singing birds comes to our land.

O let me see you,
O let me hear you;
Sweet is your voice,
Lovely is your face,
My Beloved's face.

Till the day breaks
   And the shadows fall away,
      Return and meet me there
         In the high and holy hill of the Covenant.

Beloved! Arising as the dawn
And fair as the moon;
Altogether lovely —
Beloved and Friend,
Set me as a seal close held within your loving heart;
For love is strong as death.
As the ring fits closely,
So wear me on your hand.

Many waters cannot quench your love for me,
   Your love no flood can drown;
      Giving all for your love
        I think nothing of loss.

From the Song of Solomon

6

O Lord, my heart is reaching out for that spark of life breathed forth by your Spirit. I am mindful of my emptiness without you — a cocoon, yet containing the beauty of your painted wing. I know that beauty cannot be confined. It must spread its silk to glide upon the breeze, that others seeing might marvel. Yet when they see you, are they too mindful of the ugly shell which contained you for a while?

I am that shell. You wove me around you with skill and complexity. You created me. I became aware of your beauty developing within me, as you had developed it in millions before me. You have shared with and within me personally the glory of your creation. I can serve your purpose only in the way you designed, and without you I am nothing. My relationship with you develops beyond my capacity to keep it within myself. Let me, with all who know you, marvel at your greatness.

Thank you for developing and spreading from within me that spark of life.

7

Almighty God, your majesty and beauty surround me.

I am in awe of your power and glory, for you have created all things. Nothing lives or breathes or has its being except through you.

It is you who hung the stars in place; who made the heavenly bodies to move in their appointed paths. You caused the tides to move. You created man in your image.

You sent your Son to be my reconciliation, and to draw me to you.

Thank you for choosing me to be your child and, through the shed blood of Jesus Christ, for assuring my soul of a destiny in your eternal Kingdom.

8

Thank you, Lord,
for
your gifts of bold imagination;

and people
and music
and humour
and playful recreation;
and love
and light
and life
and that innate spark
that explodes
in joyous celebration;
Thank you, Lord,
for the gifts
in your creation.

9

Dear Lord, there are billions of people on the earth, so it seems impossible that you should be aware of me. But every day, I hear the chirping of sparrows — drab, insignificant little birds. Then I am glad to read your words assuring me that your Father is aware when even one sparrow falls. Your awareness does not stop the sparrow from falling, but it tells me that the little bird has significance for you.

So, I believe that you are aware of me, and of my friends, although we may not be raving beauties, or of universal importance, or geniuses.

I thank you, and I love you, and appreciate the opportunity of speaking with you today.

10

(A mealtime prayer)

O God, our heavenly Father,
We thank you for our common table
And earth's provision for our human needs.
These are your gifts, O Lord,
Expressions of your concern for us.
Help us ever to remember how privileged we are
When together we share and partake of food and
friendship.
Hallow with your presence every common meal
And, with your blessing, each breaking of the bread:
Through Jesus Christ our Lord.

11

(On looking down upon the earth)

I'm sitting in a clear-blue world, Lord;
Was there ever anything so pure?

I'm feeling very close to you, Lord —
Nearer than I've ever felt before.

It's true I've never doubted your creation
Of a world of wonder, mystery and awe;
But here above the clouds I see it
As a panoramic glimpse from Heaven's door.

Green sea, frilled edge skirting shoreline,
Meets rocky coast and patchwork cloak of earth;
While mountains grey, but topped with snowy icing,
Are foil to clouds of wool, soft, new as birth.
I want to stay just here, above the clouds, Lord;
There have been others gripped by sudden like desire
To dwell so close to your transforming
As to environ the essentially free and high.

Good as it is just here above the clouds, Lord,
Flight still affords me yet a change of view.
I must return a new and different person,
And bring to earth the glory shared with you.

12

O greatest Love:
You knew me from the day my life began;
A single human cell beyond the scan
Of the most prying eye of any man.
     But you could see,
     O greatest Love,
     The start of me.

O greatest Love:
You shaped me from the day that I was born;

And as I took my first fresh breath of dawn,
So then began the moulding of my form.
   And you could see,
   O greatest Love,
   What I would be.

O greatest Love:
The bitter sweet of laughter and of tears,
Embroidered on the pleasures and the fears,
Of all the different happ'nings of the years
   Have helped me see,
   O greatest Love,
   What made me — me!

O greatest Love:
The mystery of all that makes me mine
Is nothing less than what you did design;
And what I am bears marks of the divine,
   So all can see,
   O greatest Love,
   You made me — me!

Sin, repentance and forgiveness

13

Gracious and loving heavenly Father, I come before you now as King David came when the realisation of his sin swept over him. 'Create in me a clean heart, and renew a right spirit within me', was his prayer. Lord, I make it mine today. I confess, Father, that I have sinned. In my selfishness and self-will I have transgressed and fallen short of your holy standard for my life. I have sinned in thought, word and deed. Truly, Father God, I am sorry.

In a spirit of penitence I come, kneeling before your throne of grace to lay there the burden of my wrongdoing. As I repent I admit, Lord, that in my thoughtlessness I have overlooked the fact that my poor attitude and untimely behaviour and even what I have said, would adversely affect others.

Forgive me, Lord. How deeply relieved I am to understand that when Jesus Christ, your pure and holy Son, was crucified, in a mystical and loving way his death dealt with all the sin of the world, including mine.

In faith I now believe that Jesus died for me, that his shed blood miraculously atones for my sins, and that I can become clean in your sight. O thank you, Lord! This is so tremendous, and restores joy into my life. Please, Lord, grant me the strength and courage to put right as far as I possibly can that which I share in secret with you now. And Lord, help me to strengthen the weak areas of my character, so that I shall not make the same mistakes again.

To you be all praise and glory! In Jesus' name.

14

Lord, you've heard me so many times before
Saying, 'I'm sorry';
Saying, 'I love you';
Saying, 'I really want to please you'.
You've then seen me so many times

Doing the same things again;
Forgetting all about you again;
Letting you down again.
What do you think of someone like me?
Can it be that you still love me?
Can it be that you still want me?
That you still desire to forgive me?

O Saviour, who returned, hands outstretched, to the very people who nailed them to a cross, help me to know that your hands ever reach out to heal and to help me; that though your heart is heavy and your tears flow in response to my failings, your love persists in its longing for me.

Lord, I am so weak. Do in my life that which I need, that of which I am incapable. So that when I next kneel before you, I might sense your joy, rather than your sorrow at the sight of me.

15

Dear Father, your love is such that you gave all that you had, that I might live, and that my life might be an abundant, happy and fulfilled one. I've been so slow to respond, to repent completely. Help me to leave not only the sin, but everything that gets in the way of my doing what is pleasing to you, even if it seems harmless and even virtuous in many ways. Forgive me for my foolishness. Man's greatest joy is to be found in pleasing you. Help me to want nothing else, and to discover that I **need** nothing else. Lord, transform me completely, that you might be in every thought I think, a part of every waking moment, a reference point in every decision made, however great or small.

16

Lord, how did that fly get into this room? The door is shut and so are the windows. How is it that so small a thing can distract me, buzzing around my head? Yet that is how temptations come. I don't go looking for them. I don't know where they come from, or how they get in. I try to ignore that little thought, but it just will not stop buzzing around in my head. Help me to deal with it before this passing traveller becomes a guest. If I cannot swat it dead, chase it from me by filling my mind with thoughts of higher things — things that will deafen me to its distracting buzz.

17

Forgive me for not praying, Lord, but it seems that sometimes it is all repetitious words that you've heard before. Forgive me when I think that you would rather hear the eloquence of others than me again. But how tired you must get, listening to me so often repeating myself.

18

Lord, I'm almost too frightened to pray, to say words that you have heard so often before.

I fail you.

I fail you in what I say and do, in the things that I **fail** to say and do. Most of all, I fail you in my attitude of mind to others, in my spirit. Your word says that 'whoever does not have the Spirit of Christ does not belong to him'.

You must be so fed up with me. I'm such a hypocrite. People compliment me, but you know the truth. They tell me I'm a lovely person, and that just makes me feel worse. They don't see the things I think or feel or harbour.

I feel so wretched, Lord. Forgive me. Forgive me and put me right with you. Give me your Spirit and a hunger for the very mind of Christ.

19

Because your love is constant, O God, I come seeking your mercy. I ask that your mercy will not only forgive my sins, but will wipe them all away. I want to have evil washed from me, and to be clean from sin — my sin.

I am fully aware of my faults, and the knowledge of my sinful words and actions is never far from my mind. All my sins have been committed against you, because it is you who have determined what is right and what is wrong. I recognise, therefore, that you should judge me, and should condemn me. From the time of my birth, sin has been part of my nature.

You require me to be sincere and truthful, and to have all my being filled by your wisdom. Only if you take away my sin, shall I be truly clean; and if you wash me, I shall be even whiter than snow. I so much long to hear the sounds of joy and happiness. I have been depressed by my sins and your displeasure, but I know I can be filled with gladness again. Please let it be as though my sin had never happened.

And now, Lord, give me purity of heart, and make all things new within me.

(Based on Psalm 51:1-10)

20

Lord Jesus, I kneel at your feet.
In faith, I see you on the cross, your body broken, your hands nailed, your side pierced.
I see your blood flow.
I hear your prayer: 'Father, forgive them, for they don't know what they are doing.'

I see you die.

Lord Jesus, you died for me.
My sins nailed you to the cross; your love held you there.
My sin brought you agony and death; your love accepted it gladly for my sake.

Lord Jesus, I confess my sin to you now . . .

I offer you no excuses, Lord.
I acknowledge my guilt.
I open my heart to you, and cast myself at your feet.
Have mercy, Lord: forgive me.

Thank you that you are more willing to forgive than I am to confess.
Help me to turn from my sin; to receive your forgiveness; to walk, by your Spirit, a path of righteousness and truth.
Thank you for your love, grace and mercy.

As I rise from my knees, I lift my head . . . I pray.
As I face life's temptations, as I face doubt and discouragement,
Go with me, Lord Jesus; and may I go with you.

In your name, I pray.

21

Lord, you know that I love you.

Whenever I recall Peter's dialogue with you at that Galilean beach breakfast, I feel as he must have felt . . . a deep longing to express my love . . . and a deep sense of guilt that I have failed, yet again, to keep my promises to you.

Forgive me, Lord.

22

I never knew, Lord, what they meant when they said the burden of sin had been rolled away. Sometimes Christians say the oddest things! But Lord, something wonderful has happened!

How can I describe it? I feel free! I feel elated! Is that putting it too strongly?

I feel as if a burden has been taken off me!

Well, there I go — saying the same sort of thing other Christians are saying.

Thank you, Lord, for my sense of having been forgiven.

23

Lord, I am not sure about the connection between guilt and health. I have heard of psychosomatic illness. I have heard that anxiety and stress can lead to physical symptoms. And I have read that often in your ministry you made a link between physical healing and forgiveness of sin. Help me, Lord, to trust you for your forgiveness.

I feel better already! There must be something in it!

Seeking the will of God

24

Almighty God, help me to discover your will . . . to love your will . . . and to do it.

Or — if that is more than I can manage — to be told your will . . . to dislike your will . . . and to do it.

25

Dear Teacher-God, take me to school,
Teach me the wisdom of the fool,
Whose foolishness is hope divine —
The thief's, the priest's, the whore's and mine.
In the sheer nonsense of his power
I place my faith — and in this hour
His choirs sing for ears that hear;
For eyes that see the night breaks clear.

So chalk upon your blackboard, Lord,
A diagram, a sum, a word,
That — reading, studying, knowledge gleaning —
I may understand the meaning
Of bloodstained nails, a final cry,
A curtain torn, a darkened sky.

And give me homework, that for me
The reality of Calvary
May stay within my self-pretension,
Engendering this one intention:
To be — through wisest love and labour —
The fool of Christ, and of my neighbour.

26

Saviour of light, I look just now to thee;
Brighten my path, so only shall I see
Thy footprints, Lord, which mark the way for me;
Light of my life, so surely thou wilt be,
   O Man of Galilee!

Another touch, I ask another still,
That daily, hourly, I may do thy will;
Healer of wounds and bearer of all pain,
Thy touch, thy power are evermore the same.
   O Man of Galilee!

Lord of my life, I dare step out to thee
Who stilled the waves and stayed the tossing sea;
When floods o'erwhelm, my safety thou wilt be;
When nightfall comes, O Lord, abide with me;
   O Man of Galilee!

Pilot of souls, I trust thy guiding hand;
Take thou the helm and, at thy blest command,
I sail straight on until, the harbour won,
I reach the glory of thy sweet well done;
O Man of Galilee!

O Man of Galilee,
Stay with and strengthen me;
Walk thou through life with me,
O Man of Galilee!

27

Father, I have, as you know, a habit of making up my own mind, and then attempting to influence yours. It's become almost a matter of course that I take my own decisions, and then with exaggerated piety ask for your endorsement. I even have the insolence to sulk when your silence makes it clear that you can't approve!

I'm going to present to you now the things that are bothering me, and about which I have to take a decision soon. I am not even going to try to influence your thinking, but for pity's sake, please influence mine!

28

Is choice a tragedy?
It seems to me
It very often is,
But must it be?
Would it be better

If I couldn't choose?
Lord, in your mercy
Teach me how to use
The precious power
You dangerously give
To choose the way I work,
The way I live.

I don't ask you
To take my gift away,
But guide me in my choices,
Every day!

29

Your will and mine
Are usually the same.
That's a relief!
There's the odd time,
When they don't coincide,
I come to grief!
I go your way,
Complaining as I go,
With such bad grace
My 'yes' is almost 'no'!
Eventually
I do what you suggest,
And later on
Discover you knew best!

Give me obedience with a smiling face,
To go unwelcome ways with better grace.

30

'These sayings ... are given as examples of a lived-faith ...
grace clearly preceding the demands they represent'
(Joachim Jeremias)

Your words, O Master, linger in my mind,
And bright with promise of your Kingdom's reign
Delineate its patterns, making plain
What is the willed intention. But I find

They will need flesh, some earthly form and place
If all that they envision is to be —
Some concrete, live embodiment in me
And, in my small world's compass, given grace.

And that's already mine, blest pledge and sign
For every inborn hope and willed intent:
Prevenient grace, it seeks to implement
And undergird each purposeful design,

Prompting to prayer and action when you call,
Destined to be the salt that savours all.

31

'Jesus said, 'My food is to do the will of the one who sent
me, and to complete his work' John 4:34, JB.
'It is God, for his own loving purpose, who puts both the
will and the action into you' Philippians 2:13, JB.

Father,
In seeking your will for me
I must learn and follow the way of Christ

who, under your divine action,
surrendered himself utterly to your purposing,
allowing your Holy Spirit to act within him
in the common ways of the everyday,
and in the high demands of his destiny,
often without knowing what the Spirit was doing,
and even being content not to know.
You alone knew
what was most profitable and expedient for him,
and in this assurance he abandoned himself
to your all-wise purpose and loving care,
accepting in faith the cross
with joy — love's vindication.

I must surrender too, O Lord,
envisage every moment as a manifestation of your will;
esteem and love the innumerable and diverse ways
you underpin and direct my life.
I need your help in trust, O Lord,
to believe that the methods you adopt
are always for the best;
and in faith, Lord, believing that
'All shall be well
and all manner of things shall be well'.

32

Dear Lord and Father, thank you for your forgiving grace,
and for inward assurance of salvation, sealed in my heart
by the Holy Spirit. What a joy it is to be held by your
almighty hand in every situation of life.

I know, Lord, that you have a plan for my life, and all I want to do is what you have willed for me. In every decision, be both my guide and my comfort.

There are so many desires and attractions that are good, but I want to know that my choices are pleasing to you. I am waiting upon you to guide and assure me concerning your will.

Here, Lord, I commit my way to you. As I read your word, I prayerfully listen for your voice in the stillness of my heart. No matter whether it be a great work or a quiet service, Lord, I am in your hands.

May the presence of Jesus be real to me, and may his Holy Spirit reveal the path before me. In his name I yield myself for guidance.

33

Dear God, you know that I have a very important decision to make very soon. I've been running the options around in my mind, trying to think my way into each of them. I've tried to do more than think: I've tried to *feel* my way in each set of circumstances. It has absorbed me totally; my mind has little room for anything else today. I'm so preoccupied with it, Father, completely wrapped up in it. And it's made me so tired. I'm beginning to wish the whole thing had never started.

Please, will you help me? Will you help me to sort it out?

Some people say you have a plan for everyone's life. I'm never too sure about that, Father, because I know some very good-living folk who have encountered experiences so devastating they could never have come from you. But if it is true, please help me to see clearly what you see as the best thing to do in this situation.

I want to know what your will is, Father; please make it clear to me by helping me to feel what is right. When I'm thinking all the options through again tomorrow, please give me a sense of peace when my thoughts and feelings correspond with your will.

I affirm my willingness to respond positively when both you and I know that I've got it right.

Thank you, Father.

34

Heavenly Father, I come to you in confidence, knowing that you are listening to me. Thank you for hearing and answering my prayers.

Help me to listen to you in these quiet moments, for I need to know your will. I do not want to make a mistake, or be influenced too greatly by my own wishes. I need to hear clearly your will in this matter, and in all my concerns.

So, speak to me, O God. Let me know your will without any shadow of uncertainty. Reassure me, as only you can, that the 'still, small voice' in my heart is giving me your message, and only yours.

Yes, Lord, help me to listen, and really to hear what you are saying — not just what I want to hear.

And since true listening involves more than merely hearing the words, enable me to obey your voice, and to follow your leading — implicitly, without hesitation, gladly, and always.

'Speak, Lord, for I *am* listening' and ready to accept your will, whatever it may mean.

35

O Lord,
If only I'd listened . . .
listened to those calmer, sweeter, gentler voices —
voices long lost,
supernally inspired.
If only I'd listened
to their cautions and godly advice,
and not thought: 'I can make it — or unmake it'.
How can I get back to what you intended me to be, Lord,
when so many years have built
their crust of cynicism, self-preservation and indifference,
and cast my mind in formulas of fear, failure and bewilderment?
God, isn't it all too late?
Yet, those precious voices still seep through this
dismal aggregation,
suggesting I might
try the 'gum tree stripping' process for myself:
that if, like this lovely tree, I peel back the outer layers of bark,
I'll come to the essential self — the better self that you made.
Not naive, and stupid, Lord; I couldn't be that —
but my intended self.
Help me to discover what you created.

36

O Lord, I think about self, and of how it creeps up into my life without my even realising all that is happening.

I do pray that you will always be on the throne of my life; any time that I try to take over, will you gently remind me that you are in control. If I fail to heed your gentle reminder, then do that which needs to be done in order that I may truly glorify you through my life.

Help me to keep my eyes focused on you and not on self — then my worry will be replaced by your presence and your peace. My feelings of inadequacy will be replaced by your strength, and the assurance that you are with me. My 'perfectionist' ways and the desire to please everybody will be replaced by one desire only — to please and glorify you.

Thank you, Lord, for emptying me of self, and for filling me with all of yourself. I love you, Lord.

37

I pray that out of your glorious riches, you may strengthen me with power through your Spirit in my inner being, so that Christ may dwell in my heart through faith. And I pray that I, being rooted and established in love, may have power together with all the saints to grasp how wide and long and high and deep is the love of Christ — and to know this love, which surpasses knowledge, so that I may be filled to the measure of all the fullness of Christ.

(Based on Ephesians 3:16-19)

Consecration and dedication

38

Dear Lord, in moments of quiet private prayer like this, I find no difficulty in totally consecrating myself afresh to you. I long to be totally absorbed within your will so that whatever talents and graces you have entrusted to me may be used entirely to make known your thinking and purposes.

But I don't live in a monastery. You have placed me here in a busy world, and it's all too easy for me momentarily to forget these precious moments of sanctity and sanctuary in your close presence when I return to that busy world.

I can't escape the demands of life. Frankly, I don't really want to. Life in a monastery wouldn't appeal to me at all. Despite all its pressures and problems, the world — your world — excites me, and I won't shrink from playing my part in trying to make it an even better place. But these splendid resolves so easily get dented, or evaporate. So how do I keep this moment of sparkling commitment fresh and unsullied when in the midst of the demands and distractions of the world?

Lord, you alternated between mountain-top experiences of communion with your Father, and confrontations with clamouring multitudes. Your composure was never ruffled. You never deviated from your dedication. You said you only did that which your Father commanded.

I now claim fulfilment of your promise to be with me always, and as you give me the sight to see the right, so I claim your strength to do it and keep on doing it.

Quick as the apple of an eye,
O God, my conscience make!
Awake my soul when sin is nigh,
And keep it still awake.

39

Dear heavenly Father, by the light of your loving me, and in the felt warmth of your presence, I want to make a commitment to new dimensions in my prayer time.

Thank you for giving me gladness in the things I try to do for you. But I find it so very hard to be still, and to listen and to wait for your guidance. The call to activity surges through me like a pulsing blood-stream. I long for action all of the time. I am restless if I am not *doing*.

Make me aware, dear Father, that my work for you will suffer if I cannot put less of myself into serving, and instead do it in the strength and with the vision that come from waiting patiently on you.

I do have a full knowledge of what I really need. Give me the willingness to receive it from your ready hand.

I promise to keep on trying.

Heavenly Father, please help me.

40

Dear heavenly Father, you have such high expectations of your children, and the command to be perfect worries me a little.

You don't seem to make allowances of any kind, Father, even though you know that goodness comes more easily to some people than to others.

I think you have known about my concern. Your Holy Spirit has led me to take note that Peter of the Gospels later became Peter of the Epistles, and I have seen that on the way he too had quite a few ups and downs.

Thank you, Father, for making it clear that it may take time for me to become what you would have me to be. Thank you for reminding me that my journey will be one of unceasing effort and constant striving. I just don't want to have to be seeking your forgiveness all the time.

I am talking to you about these things, Father, because I love you, and I do want to come up to your expectations.

I know that you will give me all the help I need.

Thank you, heavenly Father.

41

My Father, I do love you so much — yet I feel I am giving you so little. Make me, I pray, willing to be completely open to you, receptive of your love, so that I may be more perfectly formed in the likeness of Christ.

Dear Lord
　I give you myself . . .
　　　The sum of my weaknesses and of my better
　　　　　moments . . .
　　　　of my failures as well as my good intentions . . .
　　　　　of my coolness as well as my enthusiasm . . .
　　　　　　of my desire to grow — and my holding back.

I bring you my joys and my times of depression;
I bring my love for others, and those shameful times of
coolness in the face of need;
I bring you . . . all of myself! I feel such a mixture still,
dear Lord — yet there is such a longing in my heart to be
filled with your love, and transformed with the Spirit of
Jesus.

So I come again to you, my Father; it is all I can do.

Take me . . .

Fill me . . .

Use me . . .

To reflect your glory in this needy world.

In the name of your Son, Jesus, my Saviour.

42

Dear Lord, it's raining outside, and it's cold. I prefer it to
be dry and sunny. I don't like to be uncomfortable. I'd
rather be cosy and warm.

Tell me, Lord, am I like that in my spiritual warfare?
Would I rather stay in my protected cocoon of safe and
comfortable activity, than venture out into the cold and
relentless service to which your Spirit leads? If that is so,
Lord, then I am sorry.

I will prepare myself, and strengthened with your word go
out and do the task which your Spirit directs. I will speak.
I will act. Dear Jesus, make me strong.

43

Lord, be in my heart and mind, so that I can know you
    better —
  In my loving and thinking, guide me step by step.
Lord, be in my eyes and ears, so that I can know you
    better —
  In my seeing and hearing, guide me step by step.
Lord, be in my hands and arms, so that I can know you
    better —
  In my touching and feeling, guide me step by step.
Lord, be in my legs and feet, so that I can know you
    better—
  In my coming and going, guide me step by step.
Lord, be in my daily life, so that I can know you better —
  In everything and all things, guide me step by step.

44

Saviour, in accents so tender,
Thou has called me by my name;
Gladly my all I surrender
As thy promises now I claim.
Always in my heart to enthrone thee,
I submit my will to thy power;
Lord of my life now I own thee,
Sanctify each passing hour.

Faithful to thee and my calling,
Saviour, I would ever be;
Save me, O save me from falling,
In temptation deliver me.

Naught would I recall from thine altar,
All my life to yield to thy will;
If on the way I should falter,
Let thy hand support me still.

> All my heart I give to thee;
> Every moment to live for thee;
> Daily strength to receive from thee
>   As I obey thy call.
> While I bow in prayer to thee,
> I commit my way to thee;
> Here just now as I say to thee,
>   'I dedicate my all'.

45

Lord, without you
I was made of glass.
The world possessed me
and I was easily shattered.

Oh, Lord, if I could
be remade,
retaining you within,

then I am made of glass
to reflect your light;
then I am transparent
to reveal your love.

The world cannot possess me,
and I will not break again.

46

Dear Lord Jesus, I give you . . .
        my hands to do your work
        my feet to walk in your way
        my eyes to see as you see
        my tongue to speak your words
        my mind, that you might think in me
        my spirit that you might pray in me.

Above all, Lord, I give you my heart, that through me you might
love the Father, and all mankind;
I give you my self, that you might grow in me, and that you,
Lord, might live and work and pray through me.

I give to your care . . .
        my soul and my body
        my mind and my thoughts
        my prayers and my hopes
        my strength and my work
        my life and my death
        my parents and my family
        my friends and my neighbours
        my country and all the world

This day, and for ever.

47

Blessèd Lord, to see thee truly,
   Then to tell as I have seen,
This shall rule my life supremely,

This shall be the sacred gleam.
Sealed again is all the sealing,
  Pledged again my willing heart,
First to know thee, then to serve thee,
  Then to see thee as thou art.

48

O Lord, I want to be an instrument you can use, and so I commit myself — all I have and all I am — to you and to your service.

There is no hidden agenda in this dedication of my life to you. It is my glad and willing response to your accepting love for me; to your unconditional forgiveness; and to your generous giving, which enriches my life every day.

I am overawed as I ponder that you choose to work through imperfect humans. But I want to be the best I can be, for your use.

So Lord, I ask that you will continue in me the process of change you have begun. Help me not to fear these changes, but to open myself fully to your Holy Spirit, who will enable me to become the kind of instrument you can use.

Keep me ready, so you can use me at any time, and anywhere.

Keep me aware of those around me, and sensitive to their needs.

Keep me loving, so that my motivation is pure, and my service is given in your way.

Make and keep me yours, Lord, totally and for ever.

49

Father, sometimes I get glimpses of Jesus — his loving, his goodness, his strength — and they take my breath away. Deep inside, I want so much to be your person, to let you make me more and more like Jesus. That longing makes my eyes shine and my steps bounce. I want to run towards you.

I feel you calling, and I give myself to you.

I can imagine you smiling, holding out a hand and inviting me to walk with you. I'll come, Father — I'd love to come.

I don't know where you plan for us to walk. Maybe into excitement, maybe into risky territory — I'll come with you. Maybe into lonely places, maybe into paths that others can't understand — that's OK with me, too. I suppose we will walk into hard times and through pain — but I'll still come.

Lord, I don't say these things easily . . . or flippantly. But I do mean them. I belong to you, and you can take me, use me, do what you like with me.

I know you love me. I press myself into you in trust. You have never lied to me. You have never left me alone, even in the darkest times. I trust you with the parts of me that I share with no one else, with everything I care about, with even my dreams.

Father, this is me at my best — loving you and just longing to follow and to obey you. But you know that I have my other moments — even with you. Help me to keep giving myself; help me to keep following when I am not at my best. Hold my hand tightly. I can't do this without you.

50

In the quietness of this morning hour, Lord, you have spoken in a clear and unmistakable way. Whatever the trauma and anguish through which I have passed, you are still the author of my life. It is you who wrote the opening pages of the book of my life, and it is you who will pen the final chapter.

Lord, give me the serenity to accept your authorship of my life, and to trust you, no matter how painful and distressing the circumstances may be. May I, like Jesus, cry in my moment of anguish: 'Not my will, but yours!'

In the morning

51

Dear heavenly Father, how my heart sings for joy as I wake and focus on you. My mind is warmed at the knowledge that we will share this day together, and that my thoughts, actions and reactions will know the gentle and loving guidance of the Holy Spirit.

In these first moments of today, I consciously commit to you whatever time you allow me to have. I will listen intently to you with my 'inner ear', and respond with eager obedience to your direction.

Thank you in advance for making this a day which I will long remember. Thank you for sharing your glory. I praise you with my whole being, and pray in the name of Jesus, your Son and my smiling Saviour.

52

Another day, Lord, another good gift!

I don't know what you have in store for me, Lord, but I say 'thank-you' in advance because I believe that your love will be with me, no matter what happens.

Thank you for the gift of sleep, Lord, and the mystery of life returning when I wake up.

Help me to accept whatever the day may bring, even if it is unwelcome, remembering that your love can never be defeated.

Help me to do good to somebody, Lord, and to pass on a little of your love . . . could it be more than a little? Then of course it's more than I deserve!

Thank you in advance for today, Lord.

53

Lord, help me to encounter with a tranquil mind all that this day will bring.

Help me to give myself up to your will in a cheerful spirit. Sustain and support me in every hour of the day.

No matter what tidings I may hear in the course of the day, help me to accept them in a calm and resolute spirit, certain that your will is holy in all things.

Guide my thoughts and feelings in all that I do or say.

In all unforeseen circumstances, help me not to forget that all are known and permitted by you.

Help me to be straightforward and reasonable in my dealings with each member of my family, humiliating no one, and angering no one.

Lord, grant me the strength to bear the turmoil of the coming day, and all that will happen during its course. Guide my will, teach me to pray, to believe, to hope to endure and to live.

(Translated from Russian)

54

Father, I thank thee for the comforts
Of the night:
A bed to rest upon until the morning light,
Easing my tired frame;
Slumber and sleep restoring my mind,
Waking each morning refreshed to find
Another day! A new day!
Dawning for me!
Just to live for thee!
Counting my blessings I would pray,
Bless those without homes today,
Aged and worn, sad and forlorn,
Dossing beneath the arches;
Shivering, snivelling, snuggling
In boxes, blanketed in paper.
Bless those who serve them soup,
And in thy mercy hear our prayer
For them.

55

Dear God.
Help me, as I begin this day,
to be loving to everyone I meet
regardless of appearance;
to be honest in everything I do even when no one is
looking;
to be caring whenever I see a need
whether or not there is a hope of reward.

In short,
help me to be like your Son,
Jesus Christ,
in whose name I pray.

56

Lord, at the beginning of this new day, my heart reaches out to you in praise for another opportunity to start afresh.

Forgive the errors in judgment of yesterday, the little rebellions that crept in as I faced the irritations that crowded me.

Forgive the insensitivity when others demanded my time, my energies, my attention, and I wanted only to be left alone to accomplish the tasks I had scheduled for myself.

Forgive the misuse of the time I should have spent with you. Before I knew it the day was over, and I was too exhausted for more than a few verses of Scripture and a half-hearted prayer.

Help me to begin this day with you, Lord, and to be sensitive to your presence near me as I meet these same challenges. I know that they are the stuff of life, and that my spiritual walk will take me head on into them.

Help me to hold tight on to your hand, and face the day and the challenges with you.

57

New every morning are blessings abundant,
   Fresh as the dawning your love we receive;
Grace is sufficient, all needs supplying,
   This *is* your promise, and this we believe.

58

O God, our Father, I present myself before you at the beginning of this new day. I feel almost overwhelmed just in seeking to be in your presence.

Yet, as I pause and search for words to pray, I am already beginning to feel comfort. I realise that this is your own self at work in my heart, and you know how I need such inspiration to take me through the day as a witness for you.

Trinity of love and power, I thank you for the gift of your Holy Spirit, and pray that he will guide, guard and use me in all that I do this day. May those I meet see beyond me, and catch a glimpse of you and your holiness, and may my love for you be expressed in my dealings with others.

59

Thank you for your presence
   In this hour of praise;
Now receive the offering
   Of the thanks I raise.

Thank you for new insights,
   Challenging my mind;
Grant me understanding,
   Deeper truth to find.

Thank you for your healing,
   Cleansing, making whole;
Bless the new completeness
   Deep within my soul.

Thank you for your guidance,
   Marking out my way;
Give me reassurance
   For the coming day.

60

O Lord, in the stillness and freshness of this new day, I give you thanks and praise for who you are, and for all you mean to me.

Your love, your forgiveness and acceptance of me, your patience and your provision — all these draw from me a response which is impulsive and yet committed.

I offer you myself for this day, believing that you want to use me to touch other lives with your love. May this happen as you have planned. May I in no way spoil what you have in mind.

And, Lord, I ask that you will continue your work within me, for I want to attain all the potential you see in me. Help me to be helpful in this life-long process.

Make me strong in your strength today, loving through your love, and sensitive to every prompting from you.

May your plans for today, for me and for those lives I encounter, be fulfilled.

For your glory, and in the name of Jesus, I pray.

In the evening

61

Father, I'm glad to come to you at the end of the day, and spend these quiet moments in stocktaking.

Thank you for all those things which have lifted my spirits today — the glimpses of beauty, the touch of friendship, the lighthearted conversation.

Thank you, too, for the daily routine which gave a framework for my day, and a sense of stability.

Forgive me if I have spoiled anyone else's day by my wrong attitudes and actions, whether they were deliberate or simply thoughtless.

I'm so happy to end my day secure in your love. May the confidence this gives me prepare me to live well for you tomorrow.

For Jesus' sake.

62

Softly the shadows fall o'er land and sea,
Voices of evening call, speaking to me,
  Busy my hands this day,
  Small time to think or pray;
Now at the close of day I come to thee.

What can I bring to thee, fruit of today?
Have I walked worthily in work and play,
  Lightened my brother's load,
  Walking life's toilsome road,
New strength and love bestowed, Master, I pray?

As the birds homeward wend, seeking their nest,
Thou who has called me friend knowest me best;
  Forgive if I should roam,
  And grant that I may come
To find at last my home safe in thy breast.

    Lord,'tis thy tender touch now I implore;
    Day with its toil is done, labour is o'er;
    Now in the evening while shadows fall,
    Grant me thy peace, who give to thee my all.

63

Dear Father God, how readily I allow the weather to
control my moods. It was so dark and damp and cold when
I got up this morning. Everything was such an effort. Not a
smiling face to be seen; all so drab and grey.

There are times when I really don't **feel** like praising you.
Times when there isn't a leaf on the tree, not one flower to
be seen; when there isn't the tiniest break in the clouds

that would give a ray of sunshine; when the weather forecast is so grim. Those times when everything that can go wrong does go wrong, and I am struggling.

But, Lord, you have never changed. Have you failed me? Have you not rather provided for my every need? Do I **have** to have an unending supply of bright sounds and sights? Should you **have** to hand out a continuous bounty of sweets for me to believe that you are ever a good and loving Father?

Lord, shake me from my despond, and teach me how to praise you in every circumstance, believing in my heart those things which are not always evident to my senses.

64

Dear Father God, how wonderful it is to be alive today The world has been full of sunshine, joy, colour and music!

How easy it is for me to praise and worship you. Your goodness is so evident, from the flowers in the garden to the bird-song in the trees; from the corn that waves its praises in the fields to the smiles on passing faces.

Forgive me, Father, when I fail to praise you because I do not always **sense** your presence in this outward way; when my eyes are blind to the constancy of your love and provision. Help me to praise you and to worship you because you are worthy to be praised and worshipped, and not only because I sometimes feel good at your obvious presence.

65

Thank you, Lord, for this handing-over time at the end of the day.

Thank you, Lord, for time to wind down and to reflect and to pray.

I give you today . . . with its sudden joys and dulling routines, its purposefulness and its uncertainties.

Thank you, that as I reflect on today I can hand it over just as it was . . . trustfully, with a quietened heart, and a spirit made tranquil by the gifts of your presence and your peace.

66

As the end of another day shrouds itself in the dark cloak of night, I remember, Father, that you created both day and night.

Thank you for the hours of rest that restore the energies required for tomorrow. Thank you for this quiet time to reflect on the happenings of the day. Lord, I have tried to bring honour and glory to your name. I go to rest knowing that I have done my best to serve you.

The night holds no terrors for me, for I am not alone in the darkness. Thank you, Father, for the Light of Life, Jesus Christ my Saviour. I truly believe that his Spirit shines through my life, and I want others to see him in me.

Thank you for today, and all that transpired. Give me an even better day tomorrow to glorify your name.

67

The sun has just set, Lord;
Thank you for its warmth and light today.
But, Oh God, it's incredible —
Only my limited horizons have carried it away.
Beyond my vision it still shines
On brothers, sisters, children, all unknown to me,
But loved by you —
The larger portion of one family.

It will return again tomorrow
From them to me;
A shared ball of fire,
Reminder of your creativity —
But more than that,
Reminder of love's wide responsibility.

68

May thy grace and peace o'ershadow
  Those for whom we pray tonight;
May thy mighty arm uphold them;
  They are precious in thy sight.
Lord, for answered prayer we thank thee,
  Thou art good in all thy ways;
With thanksgiving we adore thee,
  Fill our hearts with love and praise.

In the busyness

69

This is going to be another busy day, Lord. There will be those times again when I start to panic, and to wonder if I can do all that will be expected of me. It is easy to say, 'But you can only do a day's work in a day'. I know that's the theory, but today there is still some of yesterday's work left, and tomorrow there will be some of yesterday's *and* some of today's. And so it goes on. You know, Lord, that I give each day my very best effort, but it seems it isn't always enough.

And yet, Lord, as I look back, I see how everything has worked out in the past. My tasks have been accomplished, there have been times when things have eased up, and your grace has provided just what was needed.

Instead of asking you to speed me up, Lord, I am asking you rather to calm me down. Let me relax in the knowledge that together, you and I can get through. Thank you, Lord.

70

Just pausing a moment to talk to you Lord;
Because I must.
Pressures are crowding in, dulling my joy.
I have so many things to do, people to see,
But I must ask for your steadying hand upon this day.

Clear my mind, help me to make right, unhurried decisions,
Ease the tensions as I breathe deeply, and look up —
Perhaps at the towering majesty of a tree;
Or look down —
Perhaps at the delicate structure of a plant.

All created things are in your hand, and I rest there
For just a moment or two,
Taking strength from you to see me through this day
With serenity and fulfilment.

71

Lord, enter my room today . . .
Not only this room of four walls, of sight, of sound, of
smell . . .
This room where I feel the pressure of my circumstances;
But enter, Lord, the inner room of my spirit
Where the real 'me' resides;
There, where fears, despair, doubt,
The inexpressible aching,
Also the ashes of my broken dreams
Hold me captive to my circumstances.

The door is ajar, Lord. . . . Enter today!
In the beautiful intrusion of your presence.
Love,
Joy,
Peace,
Will come;
The ugliness will dissolve away . . .
For you are here!
In my room . . .
Enter, Lord, today!

72

Lord, I may forget to speak to you during the busyness of this day. If I do, forgive me. Urge me to stop and contemplate my surroundings for a few precious moments — moments that so quickly fade into the yesterdays of my life.

Inspire me with strains of calming and holy thoughts that move through my mind like sweet music, when all around is chaos. Guide me through the hustle of the world with your gentle hand on my shoulder. Erase the wrinkle from my anxious brow, and grace my lips with a peaceful smile that lasts through the day.

Most of all, love me in spite of my tendency to stumble under the day's demands, and grant me an inward oasis of tranquillity where I can redeem what remains of me.

73

Mark 4.30-32

Come,
Here is a kindly country
Not far removed from city streets
Where dumb entreaty, loud complaint,
Make their demand incessantly;
Yet far enough as to ensure
Some respite from their claims and care:
A place of rest,
Invisible
Save to the inward eye.

Here
Time settles, quiet falls,
And tired spirits shed their languor.
They now may range carefree, secure
Within love's own immensity,
Sharing their Master's company
As healing virtue freshly springs
And past distress
Is rendered back
In love's own currency.

74

Psalm 46.10

'O how good it is to listen to God in our hearts,
even more than to speak to Him'
(Francis de Sales)

Seek to listen,
O my soul,
Finding in humble stillness
Here before the Lord
A place of receptivity:
Where, with inward ear attuned
To frequencies ranging far above
All fleshly sense and sound,
You may detect his whispered word
And quicken to his touch.

75

Father, you know me so well — how I always claim that I
thrive when I am in top gear. But do I really thrive — or
just survive? Jesus came that I might know life in all its

fullness — but do I? Top gear hardly allows me time to gaze into a pansy and find the cutest face, or draw in the fragrance of a rose. Busyness does not allow me to experience the fascination of a tiny child forming his vocabulary. Nor does busyness allow me to sit beside an elderly person, and be transported to the charm of a bygone era.

Each new morning, I ask you to hold my hand, but how can you if I race ahead? How rude of me to jerk *you* into *my* plans for the day! Restrain me, Father, that you and I might walk hand-in-hand, side by side. Guided, encouraged and energised by your presence, at your pace for me, I will *thrive* and not just survive. Thank you, Father.

76

Lord, this promises to be 'one of those days', with demands coming from all sides. I want to cope and to care, but I do need help.

I know that I should prioritize my tasks, as they say, and sort out those which are presented as urgent, and those which are really important. But that isn't easy, Lord!

Please save me from panic and paralysis. Help me to visualise my duties, not side by side like an advancing army, but one behind the other, in proper order, waiting for my attention.

If I am too busy to keep my appointment with you, I know that I am simply too busy. Help me, O God, to keep my life in balance, as did Jesus Christ your Son.

77

Dear Lord, the rush of the world, of daily life, is ever present! The weight of responsibility pulls in many directions.

O Lord, calm my spirit and soul so that I am able to abide in you daily, and never trust only in my own wisdom or merit.

How foolish I am sometimes! May I rely on you completely, and long for communion with you. How much richer I will then be! Help me, Lord.

In times of depression, despair and uncertainty

78

Dear Lord, I feel so depressed. I would rather not use that word; I would certainly not wish my friends to hear me say it. But I can admit it to you.

I'm not sure what makes me feel like this from time to time. It may be something definite which someone has said, or something which has happened, but I can't quite put my finger on it. Other people seem to cope all right with the same kinds of situations, but I just can't. You created me, Lord, and I suppose that for reasons best known to yourself you allow me to get depressed easily.

You know, Lord, that I sometimes live for days at a time without smiling, without enjoying anything that takes place. It is so hard to have to make conversation with people, so difficult to take an interest in life, impossible to make decisions. It is like living in a valley, with the sides pressing in.

Sometimes, I want to cry, for no apparent reason — and sometimes, when no one knows, I do cry. . . . Sometimes, I want to curl up within myself, and shut out the world. . . . Sometimes, I want to stand and stare out of a window, just looking, not doing anything — but perhaps going through so many black thoughts. . . . Sometimes, I want to go to bed and just get away from everything in sleep — perhaps hoping to sleep for ever. . . . Sometimes, I want to drive my car along road after road, going nowhere, going anywhere . . . but sometimes, Lord, I want to drive my car very fast into a wall . . . over a cliff.

We are all different, Lord, but I would really rather not be so different.

I have spoken to you like this before, Father, because you are always there to hear me. And . . . I am still here. And the good days do come. Please, Lord, just help me to be more positive when the bad days are here. I can't 'pull myself together' as they say. But you can help so much with the pulling.

At least, when I meet others with the same problem, I can identify with them, I can stand alongside them. I can be their listening ear, Father, as you are mine.

Before I say 'Amen', dear Lord, help me to say, 'Hallelujah'!

55

79

So often, Lord, I find myself asking, who are *'they'*?

When I hear about the world and its problems, someone always seems to be asking, 'Why don't *they* do something about it: provide more money, more personnel, more facilities?' Politicians say it, clergy say it, social workers say it, ordinary people say it. But who are 'they'?

Sometimes, Lord, it seems that the government is 'they'; but government leaders suggest that the opposition party is 'they'. Young people, black people, the police, foreigners, all seem to be 'they' to somebody. Many people are quite convinced that the Church is 'they', to be blamed for many of the world's wrongs.

It certainly appears, Lord, that 'they' are responsible for so much sadness in the world, so much injustice, so much inefficiency, so much anger and helplessness and heartache. You know, Lord, that in my own life there have been times when I have felt badly done by, let down, misunderstood — all because 'they' have got it wrong. I want to get matters put right, but who are 'they'? No one seems to have the answer. 'They' are just beyond reach — faceless, nameless. And yet 'they' have caused my present feelings.

Who are 'they'? Perhaps, Lord, I shall never know. But you know. And my times are in your hands.

For someone, Lord — I have to confess it — 'they' are me. For those times when I have been an unthinking, uncaring 'they' in someone else's life, forgive me, Father, for Jesus's sake.

(With acknowledgment to John Larsson, who first posed the question)

Lord, I can't even call you loving Father just now, because I no longer feel loved and I don't seem to belong to your family. I believe in you with my head — my reason tells me that everything I have learned about you is trustworthy and true; but my heart can't relate theory with reality. Nothing within me corresponds with the faith or the certainties I used to hold.

I don't need convincing that Satan is real; he constantly bombards me with doubt, discouragement and guilt-feelings. Rescue me from his taunts.

Help me to hold on to facts; to everything I've proved about your steadfastness in the past, for I can't think clearly or make any sense of life, although there is no rational explanation for the way I feel.

I never expected the Christian life to mean preferential treatment from you — favourable circumstances, constant surges of spiritual energy and enthusiasm, or perpetual euphoria that could cope effortlessly with personal pressures and other people's burdens. But I have become a stranger even to myself. My mind is in turmoil and the outlook is bleak and dark — so dark. The whole atmosphere of my life is heavy, a weight crushing my spirit. I feel isolated, and lost. I don't seem capable of loving, hoping or trusting any more. Every task, mental or menial, is such a burden that I can't make the effort to tackle it. I just want to avoid having to make the simplest of decisions. I am ashamed that I resent other people, and feel unsociable towards those who love me best. Any challenge to pray for others, or to serve in any way whatsoever, fills me with dread.

I know that prayer should be a sublime two-way communication. I accept that it is a glorious privilege to be offered access to you. But I can't seem to find any response, and I haven't the strength to ask, seek and knock until I get any satisfaction. All I want to do is give up. So often I've read that you are near to those who are at their lowest ebb; pathetic, like me. I am numb. Dear Lord, please help me to have confidence that you really are near me. In the name of Jesus I make my prayer.

81

Dear Lord, you know that I haven't even tried to read my Bible for days. Nothing in me seems to correspond with what it says, and I can't face its affirmations of victory and joy. Unless you help me, there is no hope for me. I can't bear to talk to anybody about this problem, and I certainly don't want advice. But I do want you: I need to sense your reality, to be warmed by your loving-kindness and to hear your still, small voice.

Lord, I'd like to be able to offer you strength, ability, zeal and high resolve. All I have is my brokenness of spirit, dejection of mind, heaviness of heart and a sense of utter worthlessness. I have only this unutterable weariness and sadness to offer you, but I am reaching out for you, because you gave your word that those who truly sought with all their hearts would find you. Heal me of this defeatist attitude, and help me to latch on to the promise that your strength is made perfect in weakness. I offer you full scope for your power to operate. You know that there seems to be nothing for me to live for — no future to look forward to. Enable me to see a future and a hope; make life worthwhile again, and make me know that there is a place in your plan for me. I need to feel wanted — of some value to you.

Many of your close friends have gone through a 'dark night of the soul'; if that is happening to me, then it seems interminably long, with no prospect of dawn ever breaking. Lift me out of this despair; make me stop questioning why this should happen to me. Teach me instead how you can make this adversity work out for good, and how I can learn to praise you again. Thank you in anticipation.

I dare to offload my confused thinking before you, because you, who came to bring order out of chaos, invite me to come. And I present my desperate prayer as bidden by the Lord Jesus, who loved me and gave himself for me.

82

You give me inward joy
With outward strain;
You grant me peace of heart
With pangs of pain!
When outwardly
The pattern is perturbed,
Still deep within my depths
All undisturbed,
Tranquillity holds court
And keeps her throne
When superficial joys
Are overthrown!

Not as the world gives, Lord,
Is your peace given,
Nothing on earth can shake
The peace of Heaven.

83

Dear God
You have been lonely;
Make me aware of your friendship in my loneliness.

You have been rejected;
Make me aware of your presence in my hour of rejection.

You have been hurt;
Make me aware of your healing when I hurt.

You have wept;
Make me aware of your readiness to wipe away my tears
when I cry.

When you have done this for me,
Make me aware of your love, so that I may share it with
others when they are:

lonely,
rejected,
hurt,
crying.

84

Dear God, I need you, I desperately need you. I'm so
scared and unsure of myself. But you, Lord, can lift me

from the misery of my circumstances. Please do this, Lord, so that I may again see your glory.

I need to feel the warmth of your light, to bask in its warm glow.

Comfort me, O Lord, cradle me in your strong yet gentle arms.

Shield me from harm, most of all from that which comes out of my own mistrust.

Let me be free to experience pain made bearable by your limitless grace and your abounding love.

And if I cannot see you, yet will I still trust you.

85

John 20:19; Job 36:16

Lord, I did not know you were there;
in fact, confessed surprise
that in the midst of my distress and weakness
you should suddenly break through my thoughts
with that kindly word and greeting,
'Peace be with you!'

It was what I was needing —
life in disarray, mind in turmoil.
It was my helplessness I feared.
Pain would pass,
time heal,
but loneliness and loss
Death had no right to come so suddenly!

But unbidden you came,
meeting me in my own distress:
and, oddly, it was there
in fear and pain,
I knew you understood,
you having suffered too.

Thank you, Lord.

86

To stand once more at the 'burning bush', Lord, that is my prayer. To know again the wonder and mystery of your presence, for the world is leaving its cynical stain on my soul. Its loud voices cry out, 'There is no God, there is no heavenly Father!' And there are times when doubt and uncertainty cloud my mind, and faith is delicate and fragile.

Forgive me, Father, for my doubts and uncertainties, for I once stood at that burning bush, and heard your voice, and knew for certain your presence. I have seen the mighty acts of your love and mercy. I have seen the transformation wrought by your miracles. But I am so weak, and so human. 'Lord, lift me up and let me stand by faith on Heaven's tableland.'

Grant me yet again to know that sweet intimacy of your presence. Lift my heart and soul above the crowded living of life, and take me once again to the heights of spiritual rapture. 'Unto thee will I cry, Shepherd, hear my prayer!'

87

A new environment

Lord, living takes so much energy at the moment. Every person I talk to is a stranger. Nothing has the comfort that familiarity brings. Nothing is ordinary. There are so many firsts. I get lost looking for the supermarket!

The people seem nice, but I can't help wondering what they think of me. They're probably wondering, too.

Sure, I'm excited to be here, but I feel overwhelmed, and I'm missing the people and places I've just left. So many emotions are pulling me. Will I be happy here? Will I be able to handle the job? Who will be a friend? Where will the special memories come from?

Father, you know what I'm like with no routine. I even forget to pray. But this is one of those times that remind me how much I need you. These early days need so much more energy and reserves. I need you to see me through.

Lord, please help me to relax. Help me to be myself. Save me from the burden of trying to impress. Help me to sleep. Help me to remember people's names. Help me to remember the important things in all the details with which I am bombarded. Help me not to be scared — or just help me to keep going even when I *am* scared. Help me to be warm to those around me, and don't let me focus so much on the job that I forget the people. I know we'll get there, but I could do with some reminders, please.

Father, thank you for caring friends and thoughtful people. They are life-savers. I can feel your love coming through. So much change can feel pretty lonely.

Lord, please help me to remember what this feels like. I don't want to be one of those who 'really meant to ring', or who 'kept meaning to invite you for dinner'. Help me to be aware of those around *me* in transition, too.

HOME, FAMILY AND COMMUNITY

Those in our home

88

Dear Lord, I do thank you for the privilege of my home. There are so many good things about living in this house, which is such a haven of stability in the company of those I love.

It is a warm and secure place to go out from each day, representing calm and comfort when the workaday life brings all kinds of unexpected situations. I thank you, Lord, that the well known and familiar rooms remain and wait for me until my return. More than once, Lord, they have become a place of refuge from 'out there'.

I thank you that when we as a family get together in the evening or the weekend, we can be at ease in one another's company. Sometimes there is conversation; sometimes there is quiet; sometimes there is disagreement and difference in our points of view. But we have passed through many of the same experiences together, and I thank you, Lord, because these have given us an understanding of each other that no one else can have.

Help us each to be supportive of the other, Lord, and in particular help me to be an encourager and more appreciative of the contributions which others bring to my home. May my own offering be given willingly and well, as a token of sincere thanks for the blessing of home and family. In Jesus' name I pray.

89

Lord, we each have burdens, concerns and cares. Even the smallest children have their own worries, and things that upset them. Please help them to learn what is meant by trusting you. You know that I am a natural worrier. Help me to leave all my troubles with you, and to set my family an example. May they learn that even if things do not work out the way they planned, they always work out for the best if they are handed over to you.

90

Lord, I think I know my family well, but you know what I cannot see. I bring to your their problems, hopes and dreams; the things about them that disturb me; the things about them that distress me. Yet I would not forget to praise you for the many joys they bring to me, the things they have taught me, and the things we have been through together.

Take care of them, and make them aware of your love and my prayers.

91

Dear Lord, what you've done in my life is unbelievable, tremendous, more than I could have ever dreamed of. But I'm not without trouble, trials or tears. My family doesn't seem to understand. I'm a tolerated novelty. They smile as though sorry for me, or they get irritated by me, or angry with me. I sometimes have to keep my mouth firmly closed with regards even mentioning anything to do with you, and it hurts.

Please give me your wisdom, patience and love. Speak to those whom I love, for I know that they are dear to you as well.

92

It's ever so hard, Lord. I come home from worshipping you, and my heart is bursting with what I have experienced, but my wife* doesn't want to know anything about it. She* tolerates my 'religion' as she calls my relationship with you; she sometimes gives me a lift to the church, or collects me when the service is over, but she doesn't even want to discuss you.

She thinks she knows it all, and that I have been brainwashed, that the Christian life is for the ignorant and inadequate. Lord, I do love my wife, and she loves me, but there is something missing, a loneliness in our relationship, a gap across which we don't meet.

Lord, touch my wife, show her what she is missing. I can never convince her, but you can, Lord. Help me to believe that, even when I can't feel it.

*as appropriate

93

Father God, your home is everywhere, and wherever we make our home you are there. We thank you that Jesus lived as part of a family, and learned from experience the value of mutual care and dependence.

As we make our home under the same roof, help us to share each other's hopes and fears, joys and failures — and to sense your protection and security.

Help us to be sensitive to each other's needs, and to avoid giving unnecessary pain and anxiety. May we always be ready to identify with one another, reminding ourselves of your willingness to accept us as your children.

As we live together, may we seek to understand, support and know one another better. Most of all, we ask you to share our home and make it a place where faithfulness and trust, honesty and love unite us in your care.

94

My thoughts are broad and deep with regard to my intercession with you, Lord, for those in my home. Sometimes I find it difficult to be specific with you, as thoughts and emotions tumble over each other, and I seek to achieve some priority in presenting my prayer to you.

I ask that all who share this home will feel a true sense of family unity and togetherness, yet at the same time retaining their individuality and privacy. Please, Lord, help us to recognise each other's needs for time and space to be ourselves. Help us also to share willingly and joyfully, not only the good gifts you have given us, but also the problems which inevitably come our way.

I ask that all who spend time in this home will feel your presence, hear your voice, and be aware of the outworking of your will.

In the name of Jesus I make my prayer.

95

Dear heavenly Father, it is with joy that I come into your presence. Thank you for your love for me, for the evidence of your activity in my life and circumstances. Thank you for assuring me of your power and presence through your Holy Spirit's movement in my heart and in my mind.

I have to confess that I don't always practice what I preach, but in my confession, I pray for courage and grace to be what I claim to be. Here in my home especially, I pray that my family will see me to be always reliable and helpful. I know that my loved ones look to me for comfort and assurance, and in your strength and by your grace I want to be an honest example of your love.

My family's needs are great, and at times I see them struggling with the issues that life presents. My heart goes out to them, wanting so much to struggle for them, yet knowing that I can't. I pray that they will look to you for wisdom to make the right decisions. Give them a great desire to lean totally on you. Speak to them with a strong voice, reminding them of your righteousness and of your standards for holy living.

I pray for them, that they will find hope in your word and joy in your will. I pray that you will give them a clear vision of what you want them to do and to be. Through my life, may it be easier for them to remain in your love. In Jesus' name I pray.

Absent members of family

96

Lord, we thank you for all those who are linked with us through the ties of human relationship. Some members of our extended family are separated from us by many miles, and their personal circumstances are so diverse. In our prayers, we remember them all, especially those who are ill or in sorrow, and those who may be facing temptation or passing through times of special difficulty. We know that the resources of your love are beyond our imagining, but we also know that you can meet the needs of those we remember today. We ask that your divine aid be given to them.

For any who continue in sin, or who have fallen from grace, we pray that your Holy Spirit may continue his gracious work of conviction and correction. These prayers we ask in the name of Jesus.

97

O God, source of our lives, and our constant help, we pray for those members of our family who have left this home to continue their various callings in the world. Although they are separated from us, we know that they, like us, are within the orbit of your Fatherly care. We ask that just now they may be made aware of your grace and guidance, and that this knowledge may continue with them throughout today and every day. We especially mention by name ....

98

Our heavenly Father, we thank you for the joy you have given to this home through our family relationships; for the love, nurture and discipline of family life. We pray that by faith in Jesus your continuing grace may sustain and strengthen us all.

We especially remember those who are now absent from our home, and in particular we think of .... We ask that they may be aware of your continuing presence with them. Heighten their joys, support them in their sorrows, and give them wisdom in face of perplexities. Grant them, according to your will, material and physical blessing to enrich their lives. May they live in obedience to your revealed will, and thus enjoy spiritual health, and be kept in the way that leads to eternal life.

99

Strong Father, you have made us, and we belong to you. I pray for .... who is away from home at this time. My routine continues unchanged, yet there is a sense

of loss which does not go away. I'm glad that
.... has new things to see and experience,
and that, as he/she does, so your protection and care are
always vigilant. Surround .... with your
great love, and keep us all under your protection.

You are not bound by time or distance, and so with
confidence I pray for .... Please help to
ease the anxiety I feel in those moments when he/she
seems so far away. May he/she find in the new experiences
of life the stability which can come only from you.

I have a range of false fears that surprise even me! How
could I think so much of myself and my feelings, when
everything for me is familiar and known. I'm sorry, God. I
do have confidence that you accompany ....
just wherever he/she is.

100

Lord God, I'm worried.
I would like to think it was 'concerned' . . .
but I'm worried.
I can't concentrate — even on the familiar.
I know I'm not giving attention
to the people here I love.
Restore some calm,
for I want to release .... to your care,
and be able to pray
not for my own needs,
but for ....'s.

101

Dear Lord Jesus, on this quiet Sunday afternoon, I want to sit in your presence and think about the absent members of my family. When I am with them in their homes, their needs are so pressing, and I feel so intensely their unhappiness and their joys. I imagine the worst if the breadwinner is late when driving home. I stay awake into the small hours until the teenager has safely returned. I constantly go to look for the younger child walking home alone. The dark shadow of their fears of redundancy, shortage of money, illness or accident falls upon me. But when I am absent, I trust them to life and to you. There is a detachment, yet my love is always there, and I *want* to pray for them.

Please show me how I can support them in prayer: the young, of whose lifestyles and values I know so little; and the elderly who so bravely and independently conceal their troubles. There are the distant relatives I seldom see, and the god-children on whose behalf I made such solemn vows, which I confess I have fulfilled so inadequately. Please help me to pray imaginatively for them, and ever to persevere in remembering birthdays and anniversaries. Let me add my congratulations for new babies, and for successes in examinations and driving tests — even, and especially, when there is no reply to my letters. When we do meet together on special family occasions, may we find time to listen to each other, and dare to talk about *real* things. We need your help if we are to trust each other enough to share life's unfulfilled hopes and broken relationships, as well as its good experiences.

Please make me sensitive to times when a kindness is needed, be it a telephone call, an overnight stay, a lift in my car, some child-minding or parent-minding, a hospital visit, a little financial help or a surprise gift.

Help me to be what others need in their idea of 'family', just by being there. I am part of a shared heritage, with a common name, kinship network and childhood memories. My life is part of the family history. I believe that through you I have an unconscious influence. My faith matters to each of them. How I cope in adversity matters to them. The contact I maintain with them matters. Help me above all to be ready to share my faith in ways that you will show me, and at times that you will give.

Dear Lord, bless them each *now,* even as I talk to you, and thank you for them. Lift their hearts with your love; touch their hearts with your grace, and hold them in your safe-keeping.

102

Father God, how wonderful it is to be a member of your family, enjoying the privileges which that belonging brings. Your love, your constant presence, and your patience are new every morning and evident throughout the day.

As a family, we have valued this evidence of your care, and have endeavoured to pass on the reality to our children. Now, Father, they are pursuing their chosen vocations, they have left the security of home to achieve further education and employment. I would especially ask you to have the children in your loving care. The university, the workplace, the world, are fraught with so many pitfalls for the unwary, and I would pray you to keep these loved ones in time of temptation. Help them to choose the right way, especially under pressure. Guide them in decision-making, comfort when life is difficult, and above all help them to remember the Christian values that have been taught them in this home.

Sometimes, Father, the distance is a very real problem, and it would be wonderful to see them. Thank you, however, for our modern communications services, which help to keep that personal contact. A voice on the telephone, the arrival of a letter or a fax means such a lot.

I commit the children to your care, knowing how true is your promise, 'I will never leave you nor forsake you'. Help me to trust you, and to be an encourager, as we keep in touch. In your dear Son's name my petitions and requests are made.

Parents' prayers

103

Dear heavenly Father, we bring our children to you to be blessed.

Help them to find peace with you by trusting in Jesus for salvation.

May their lives be full and rewarding, but neither so full nor so rewarding that there is no room for you.

We ask that they might have compassion and love for their neighbours, and will never forget that Jesus is the only way to God.

Give them the knowledge to understand that true wealth is that which is stored in Heaven.

May they always seek first your Kingdom and your righteousness.

We praise you and thank you for the joy we know because we belong to you.

We pray in the name of Jesus.

104

Lord, we brought him* up like we did our other children. We taught him your way, and tried to be an example to him. Why then is he* so hostile to us? Why does he reject you? When he comes home, it is as if a dark cloud has descended upon our home, and when he goes out I almost sense the house itself sigh with relief. The aggression, the arguments over nothing . . . why?

I feel so guilty.

I feel as though I have failed, although I don't know what I could have done to stop it getting like this. He seems to hate us all. The only time there is any sign of tenderness is when he wants something, or is 'using' us.

Dear Lord, daily we plead the same prayer, daily we weep for our child. I cannot see any way that he could ever change, ever respond to you; but I do believe that you still love him and that you can do the impossible.

Sometimes I feel like giving up on him. I wonder if I still love him, he's hurt me so much. My feelings are numbed. Teach me never to give up loving, praying, pleading, longing. Teach me what to say and what not to say when he's around. Help me to realise too that all I see and hear might not be the whole story of what is going on inside him.

*or her, she, or plural as appropriate

105

Lord, you have entrusted young lives to us for a short time.

Help us to be sensitive to their needs, and consistent in love and discipline.

Make us attentive listeners and grant us the gift of discernment, that we may understand their world and their concerns.

Above all, help us to show you through the example of our lives. Let your Holy Spirit reign in our home, giving us wisdom and love within this family which will spread to those around us.

Thank you, Lord, for the privilege of being parents. Teach us the responsibility, and let us be wise in your strength.

106

Lord, you've given us this new little life.

Our senses fluctuate between 'Wow!' and 'Help!'

We can't quite overcome the feeling that we're the brightest people in this universe, and yet, when we look at .... we're reduced to jelly!

Why is this, Lord? Why these emotions on a see-saw? Is it right to feel like this?

We tremble with the responsibility. This child is *ours!* Ours to shape and to guide.

And to instill values? O Lord, are our values good enough? Are we wise enough to guide anyone? Are we capable of shaping a life to go on into the future?

We're praying now that you will guide us — show us what to do — help us to keep in constant touch with your Spirit, your word, and your people — so that we keep priorities straight as .... grows up.

And lest we become too solemn and self-righteous, Lord, remind us that .... needs a sense of lightness and laughter in his/her early years, to develop a sense of trust and happy confidence.

107

Our Father, we pray for our children.

Although they're grown men and women, we see them still as lives given by you, and our love reaches out to them.

In this place of prayer, where physical distance is eliminated, we feel near to them.

We thank you for them.

We pray for their physical well-being. That's important to us, Lord. After all, we're physical beings, and we need our health.

We pray for their mental health, too. There are plenty of influences around today which would lower their appreciation of good and lovely things. Be with them, Lord, in their seeing and in their understanding.

But most of all we pray for their spiritual well-being — for their relationship with you. May their faith be soundly based, their discipleship real, and their spiritual life vital.

And may they breathe to others the love, joy and peace which are the fruit of your Spirit's indwelling.

Be with them Lord.

108

Our Father God, we praise you for your loving care of our family, and especially for your wonderful generosity in the gift of a little child. You have entrusted him/her to our care. What a great responsibility this is.

As we look into this new little face, we see potential for the future, and so much of the future of our child will depend upon us. We acknowledge this, and so we dedicate our child to you. We will need your help and guidance as we set out on the task of caring for him/her. We will need such wisdom and patience and love each day, as we seek to meet physical needs, and at the same time set foundations for the whole of life.

Help us to be consistent in our own Christian living, and it is our prayer that our example will be such that .... will find it easy to love the Lord Jesus, friend of little children.

With joy and gratitude in our hearts, here within our home we dedicate our child to you. In the name of Jesus.

Young people's prayers

109

Dear Lord Jesus, more than anything else, I need to remember that today you will never be far from me. There will be times when this will be an encouragement for me, and other times when it will serve as a warning about my actions, my words and my attitudes.

When I am tempted to do wrong things, help me to look to you for strength not to do them, and to do positive good things instead. Help me not to do anything which I would be ashamed to do if you, or even my family, were right beside me in person.

Help me not to say anything which might be offensive or rude to others, whether they are adults or young people like myself. Let me hesitate and have second thoughts before I say something which might be amusing to me, but hurtful to another person. It is so easy to show off at someone else's expense, and leave them discouraged or angry or tearful.

Help me to have respect for all people and their views, which might be quite different from mine. I especially ask that I shall be ready to learn from those whose experience of life is so much greater than my own, even if they find it difficult to communicate with me in the language of today.

When I feel lonely or misunderstood, help me to trust you, knowing that you are there, sharing in my disappointments. With you, I need never be afraid.

Please, Jesus, be my ever-present friend.

110

Father, being young isn't easy, and I need your help.

Help me to discover who I really am, and what you want for me.

Help me to get on with other people — my parents, my teachers, other adults, my friends, and especially those people I don't really like.

Help me to know the truth — the truth about you, the truth about right and wrong, the truth about your plan for my life and future.

Help me grow into a mature adult without ever losing the joy and freshness of youth.

Help me to use my money wisely, to spend it carefully, to avoid the trap of constantly wanting things, and to remember my responsibility to the poor and hungry.

Help me to resist the pressure just to act and to think as everyone else does. Give me guidance and courage so that I can make the right decisions for my life, even when those decisions might cause me to be unpopular.

Above all, help me to discover the presence and reality of Jesus for myself. I thank you, because I know that he was once a young person, and that he understands all the difficulties and challenges of youth.

In his name I pray.

111

Dear God, I want to be an individual, and sometimes the world tries to suppress me with its own ideas of what is right and what is wrong.

Please help me to be true to my own self, and to your commands.

Give me the courage to be different, and the strength to be me at all times. Give me the voice to refuse conformity, where it is not within your will, and through my individuality may the world see your light.

112

Lord Jesus Christ, please hear my prayer,
And show me how to truly care;
That what I do and what I say
May help someone today.

Lord Jesus Christ, please hear my prayer,
And teach me what it means to share;
That I will not act selfishly
To those with less than me.

Lord Jesus Christ, please hear my prayer,
And let my attitude be fair;
That if my friends be right or wrong,
They'll find my friendship strong.

Lord Jesus Christ, please hear my prayer,
And make me keen to do and dare,
That I may stand for what is true,
And do my part for you.

113

Dear Lord,
I want to be like you.
I want to serve you with a willing heart.
I want to love you with my whole heart.

But there are things in the world that tempt me,
and confuse me, and draw my attention away from you.

Forgive me when I am distracted
by the sights and sounds of the world.
Help me to follow Jesus —
to live as he did,
to love as he loves me.

In his strong name I pray.

114

Heavenly Father, I can smile with you now — smile at the foolish notion of many younger men and women, a notion that once I had. It is the idea that to be useful one has to be young. I used to think that when arthritis stiffened my joints, and wrinkled flesh masked my natural good looks, and lazy lungs forced me to slow down, then I would have to retire (with honour) from active Christian service. Silly me! Nothing could be further from the truth.

For years I have known what Jesus meant when he said that God is Spirit and must be worshipped in spirit and truth. But now I also know that you can be *served* in spirit. Thank you for teaching me this lesson, for it is of vital importance for one who is sometimes not able to do a great deal for you in a physical way.

When, for one reason or another, I am housebound, I can still stride out in prayer and wage war on your behalf against the awesome forces of darkness. And, in the same way, I can run races, climb mountains, fight wild beasts and defend lonely outposts.

Sometimes the thought comes to me that I am doing more for your Kingdom now than ever I did when I was dashing around here and there in your service. And sometimes I think that Jesus knows exactly what I mean, even though he gave his life for all mankind at the age of thirty-three.

In his name I pray.

115

Eternal God, looking back over the years of my life I can do no other than lift my heart to you in thanksgiving. As it was with the psalmist, so it has been with me — your goodness and mercy have followed me all the days of my life.

It is true there have been times of sadness and tears, difficulty and problems, perplexity and anxiety; but always you have been with me. You have comforted, supported and strengthened me.

Thank you above all for the continuing experience of your everlasting love, which has been made real to me through our Lord Jesus Christ. Amen.

116

Lord Jesus, you are the same yesterday, today and for ever. When I was young, you gave direction to my life. When I was middle-aged, you guided and encouraged me. Now I have reached the later years, you are still with me, since you have promised, 'Lo, I am with you always'. When I am feeling lonely, anxious and afraid, help me to remember that this is so, and to hold on to my trust in you.

Thank you for hearing and answering my prayer.

117

Father God you know that I now find it difficult to do things I once did easily. The passing of the years has had its effect upon me, bringing weariness of body, mind and spirit.

But still today, as when I was younger, I find encouragement in your promise, 'They that wait upon the Lord shall renew their strength'. Grant that as I become more and more conscious of my own weakness and frailty I shall be increasingly aware that I am being strengthened by the might of your Spirit in my innermost being.

This I ask, remembering that your strength is made perfect in weakness.

118

Freshen my spiritual life,
Breathe thou within my soul,
Strengthen my inner being
With holy energy and impulse.
I cannot *do* as much,
But I would *be* for thee
A living testimony
Of thy saving grace.

Those who live alone

119

I don't need to tell you who is praying, do I, Lord? When a prayer comes from this house, you know it must come from me. Who else would it be? Last week, and last month, and last year I was here alone. And next week . . . and next month . . . . and next year?

People around think I am so independent, so strong, so self-sufficient. What I am is God-sufficient. But I thank you that this sufficiency knows no limits — no limits imposed by weakness, or despair, or loneliness.

I would rather not have to spend so much time on my own. I hear the neighbours welcoming their family and friends, and sometimes they are so noisy. Inside, I grumble a little, but when the children's shouting and the grown-ups' laughter has stopped, I almost wish it would start again.

You know how much I like the sunny days, the dry days. I can go out for a walk, and once more become part of the community-family. But look at it today, Lord, pouring with rain. Nobody out on the streets, nobody at home next door, no visit from the postman. Television is helpful, but it isn't real people, is it — people I can talk to, that I can have a conversation with?

Well, now, they say prayer is listening as well as speaking. What would you like to say to me?

Good health? Oh, yes, I can't complain, for my age.

Happy memories? Absolutely marvellous! When I think of all the lovely folk I have known, the places I have been, the things I have done, the kindnesses people have shown me, the books I have read . . . no end to the memories, Lord.

Your place in my life? Even now I rejoice in wonder at the way you came to me with saving grace; the way you have always been there to give me a lift when life has been tough; the way you have so often pointed me in the right direction when I have spoken to you, as I speak to you now. The way you are still here when all the others have gone.

The strength you have given from the Bible? Truly a word for all seasons — for all my seasons, anyway. Thank you, Lord, for all that your Spirit has said to me through the Scriptures — rejoicing with me, despairing with me, chastising me, uplifting me, challenging me.

Next time I start to feel sorry for myself, Lord, being lonely, let me remember that my loneliness can never compare with yours at that awful time when you cried out: 'My God, why have you forsaken me?' Thank you for knowing about loneliness, Lord, so that you can come alongside those of us who sometimes get a bit depressed about it. You and I together will find plenty to do to keep us busy! I'm going to start by counting my blessings. If you need me, Lord, you know where I am. Still here, still alone, but with a 'Hallelujah' in my heart!

120

Father, bless those who suffer
In solitary confinement,
Sometimes for years,

Albeit for life.
So much I love to talk,
So oft I long to walk
in friendly company.
Alone they sit and wait . . . and wait . . .
And wait . . . and wait . . . and wait.
Thoughts just go round and round,
Emptiness in cell and brain.
Father, deliver us from evil,
Either to imprison or be imprisoned.

121

Lord, my partner is now there in Heaven with you, and here am I, alone where we lived together.

It's a little hard for me to give thanks as I turn the key in the door. But I take courage, and thank you for the past lovely years of sharing and caring and fellowship.

I give thanks for the promise of **your** presence wherever I am, and know that I am not alone.

Help me to reach out in love to those others who desperately miss someone who is no longer there. May they and I feel you to be doubly near to us. May we learn to look Heavenward, and be fitted for the day when we too will take residence in the mansion prepared for us in your Kingdom.

122

You have told us, Lord, not to let ourselves become burdened by anxiety. I find this hard, as we all do, Father; but by exercising daily faith I do know that you will make provision for all my needs, for all my circumstances. As a Christian, I have learned to be content (well, fairly content) with what I have and where I am.

But it isn't me that I'm most anxious about, Lord, it's some other people — people who lie heavy on my heart, who cause me hours of concern, whose choices and lifestyle seem to lead them into such troubled waters. They seem to be so far from you, so far from any source of inward strength. Some of them are obviously in great difficulty; it is there on the surface. Others seem to be having a great time in life, but I know — and you know, even better, Lord — that this isn't really the case.

These folk who cause me to be anxious: people that I see often in my daily round; people that I read about and hear about and see on television; people that I call my friends; most of all, those in my family, for whom I have a very deep love: I bring them to you now, Lord, in secret. Their names, and the care I have for them, are written only on my heart. And just now, Lord, I am going to tell you about them ....

Thank you for listening to me, Father. I pray that together we might be able to help them. It will probably have to be more you than me, Lord. I am only anxious about them because of what I think are problems, but you really know them. At least I have shared my anxieties with you. Please help me to keep loving those we have spoken about, in the same way that you love them. And to love them for Jesus' sake, not mine.

123

Dear God, my heart is breaking today with the burden I have for so many. I've grieved in your presence many times for my wayward children. I've shared with you my concern for elderly family members, and for difficult in-laws. I've told you all about the problems I have at work, with the boss and with co-workers.

Today, I read articles in the newspaper about the homeless, about crime and drugs, and about government officials who brought shame upon themselves — and about war!

Lord, I know you told us not to worry about anything, but where are you in all of this? How can I trust you to answer prayers for family and friends when the whole world seems to be falling apart?

(A time of silent meditation, perhaps looking at God's creation, is indicated here.)

Thank you, Lord, for speaking to me through your creation. Thank you for reminding me that you make all things beautiful. The ugliness of life does not come from you. I know now that I really can trust you for the best.

With this perspective, I can thank you for giving humans a free will in making choices. I gladly choose to follow your leading. Help me to understand and be patient with those who have not yet made that decision. Teach me how to show love and concern in all my relationships.

Your word says all things work together for good to those who love you. I believe this means for *your* good, for *your* purpose. I love you enough to allow you your way in every situation, because I believe it will eventually bring you glory, and some day I hope to live in the glory of your presence.

Forgive me for my doubts. Increase my faith. And help me to bring your healing into all my troublesome relationships. It helps when I remember that your Son, Jesus, had people-problems too. It is through him that I pray.

124

Dear gracious God, I approach you with an overwhelming sense of inadequacy right now. And I thank you, Lord, for understanding me and the anxiety I am feeling, even as I come to you. I feel helpless. I have no ability to control this situation; so I need your wisdom, your confidence, your peace bestowed within me.

I confess my inability to be tolerant. I have not been accepting or sensitive. In fact, I have to confess my resentment and anger.

I have also failed in my trust. I know that you are able to move and cause your will to prevail – but I also know that you need me to be your instrument.

And so, Lord,

> I seek your forgiveness. You can heal this relationship,
>   if I allow you to.
> I seek your patience. You understand me, and my need
>   to see something happen to bring about change.
> I seek your peace, because I'm really getting anxious.
> I seek your discernment, because I really must do and
>   say the right thing.
> Most of all, Lord, I seek your intervention through the
>   Holy Spirit. I just do not have the answer.

In faith, I turn this matter over to you. I seek your forgiveness, and in faith accept what you shall choose to do.

If you want to use me to bring about resolution, I am available. Do just what you desire.

I pray this in faith, confidence and your promise of victory.

125

Oh, Lord, you know how difficult it is for us sometimes to understand what is happening in the lives of those who are dear to us. We want to believe that you are in control and aware of all that is happening, and yet we are afraid. Thank you for inviting us to bring our anxieties to you.

As I kneel before you, so aware of my own inadequacies, I place in the palms of your compassionate outstretched hands that one for whom I am so concerned today. In doing so, I recognise that your love so greatly exceeds my own.

Awaken my sensitivity to any means by which you desire to use me as an instrument of your love in ministering to the burden which is on my heart.

I dare to ask my prayer in the name of him upon whom we can cast our care, because he so greatly cares for us, your Son Jesus.

Those who mourn

126

Today, Lord Jesus, there are children who have become fatherless and motherless. Families are grieving because someone has died. Whilst we believe and rejoice in the resurrection, it still hurts to say farewell. Lord Jesus, I bring these people to you now.

You know what it feels like to mourn. You wept when Lazarus died. Sometimes, Lord, it's difficult to find words for expression. But then, words are not always necessary, are they? As tears are shed, as regrets surface, as memories are revived, as the storm of sorrow seems to overwhelm — Lord Jesus, come with the touch that only you can give.

May your comfort be like a cloak around all who mourn. May they be drawn into the warm embrace of your love. In your own precious name I ask it.

127

O God, our loving heavenly Father, I want to pray just now for all who mourn the passing of a loved one or friend.

Help them to be thankful for every good thing in the life of the one who has departed.
Help them to rejoice in the love shared with the loved one, a love which is but an echo of your own great love.
Help them to be glad that those who have accepted your offer of eternal life will now be sharing a much wider and deeper experience of that love in eternity.
Help them to maintain and develop faith in the face of this crisis and to find spiritual and physical resources in you.
Help them not to live only with memories of the past, but to look to the future with hope and trust.

Thank you for the promise, 'Blessed are those who mourn, for they will be comforted.' I ask that your presence may come to all who are suffering loss in this way.

Comfort them by encompassing them with your Spirit, whom you sent to be our Comforter.
Comfort them by the shared nearness of other loved ones and friends.
Comfort them by the awareness of the love of other Christians, and may the fellowship of all the members of Christ's body be especially real to them.

I pray particularly for those whom I know to be grieving at this time:.............................. Guide me in being sensitive to their needs, so that I may say the words that will help, and leave unsaid those that will not, and above all enable me simply to be a comfort by my presence and practical help.

I remember the promises in your word:
  'I am the resurrection and the life',
  'I will not leave you comfortless',
  'I go to prepare a place for you'.
May these promises be fulfilled in the lives of us all.

Especially I pray that you will uphold the recently bereaved through the many transactions and transitions which need to be made at this time. And may they and their needs not be forgotten when these early days are past, since for them it may seem that life will never be bearable again. May new and close relationships be formed which will help to fill the void.

And help us 'so to number our days that we may apply our hearts unto wisdom.' For Jesus' sake.

Those who are ill

128

Dear Father, I come to you with prayer for those who are known to you and to me, and who are far from well at this time.

Whichever shall be your will, Lord, heal them or give them grace to bear their illness with patience. Your Son at Calvary bore such great suffering for our sakes; and I pray that he shall be alongside those in pain just now, sharing mystically with them in their burden.

I especially pray for those who have illnesses for which there is no cure at present. Make them serene, and give them confidence in your strengthening and saving grace. Let them know in their hearts that there is a life prepared for them, where pain shall be no more. May all who minister to them in body, mind and soul be granted a special measure of wisdom.

For those close to me who are ill, I ask that I shall help to make this one of their better days, by being cheerful, thoughtful and encouraging when I am with them.

In the name of Jesus, I pray, who suffers still with the sufferings of his people.

129

Dear Father, I come to you in the name of Jesus, the great physician, for those who are ill. As people once brought to him their sick and disabled in Galilee, so I bring into your presence those for whose health I am deeply concerned.

Just when they most need to pray, they themselves may find it most difficult to concentrate on you. When this happens, help them to rest in your presence, and allow your love and peace to enfold them. Make them aware of your everlasting arms of comfort when they are in pain and afraid.

To those in hospital, finding the situation hard to accept, give grace to co-operate with those who are working for their benefit. Help those being looked after at home not to feel humiliated because they have to rely upon members of the family, and have to forfeit their independence for the time being. Give patience and understanding on all sides, and let your love and gentleness guide everything that is said and done.

Whether the illness is brief, or long-lasting and serious, please bring something positive out of the suffering, transforming it into a means of spiritual progress and a deeper compassion for others. Above all, save from self-pity and complaining, by bestowing the gift of thanksgiving in all circumstances. Remind them that in all their afflictions, you are afflicted, and that Jesus himself cares about their anguish. May they discover a mystical fellowship of suffering with him. Lift their human experiences into the dimension of your eternal purpose and glory.

Thank you for those who are showing signs of improving health. Help us always to remember that your healing is for the whole person, and that you have ways of answering prayer far more perfectly than we know, even when our specific requests are not granted.

Please undertake for the other complications that accompany ill-health — tasks unfinished, worrying gaps in domestic income, disturbances in the lives of young children because of a parent's illness. May the sufferer leave all anxiety with you, until strength enough returns for the normal way of life to be resumed. And support those relatives and colleagues who have to take on additional burdens until the emergency is past.

These things we pray through Jesus, the wonderful healer.

130

Our Father, when we are forced to contemplate the mystery of illness, our faith is under fire, and we don't know any more what to believe. Thank you for the Gospels in which we see that Christ was *for* the sick, and *against* the sickness. From this, we learn that *you* are on the side of the sufferer, and that comforts us.

Into your presence, then, by our prayers, we feel we can bring the people we know who are suffering, mostly through no fault of their own. If they have to battle with doubt, be with them in the battle. If they are fighting pain, please fight it with them. In their struggle against ill-health, let them know that you are their front-line supporter. Make them sure of your presence and your peace.

For the sake of Jesus.

131

Great Physician, we feel you near — 'closer than breathing, nearer than hands and feet.' And even for this gift of suffering we thank you. You, who suffered the ills of the whole world in your body and heart, have risen triumphant, full of grace and glory. Thank you, because in our suffering we share more fully with you than when we are well. We know that 'our Lord comes, and will not be silent'. Your tears mingle with ours, your voice echoes our groans.

And on those occasions when we cannot hear you or feel you near, when it seems our crying falls on deaf ears, help us to remember that you have not forgotten us — that you have promised to 'preserve our tears in your bottle'. We wonder what purpose our tears serve, but by faith accept that they are precious to you. Strengthen our faith in times of silent suffering. Help us to know that in your economy, nothing is wasted.

We affirm our faith in your sovereign power, and claim our healing in your time. Time locks us into its narrow channel, but you, Father, see beyond time — and you are working for our good. We give you praise through our pain, knowing that 'the chains that seem to bind us fall powerless behind us, when we praise you'.

In the name of Jesus Christ, our healer.

132

O God of all love and compassion, I bow in your presence. I know your power is still the same as in the days when Jesus healed all manner of sicknesses — and I am aware of miracles of healing today. Lord, you understand the pain, the despair, the frustrations of illness, and the anxiety of family and friends. We pray, therefore, that we might have a greater faith in your power to heal.

May the one I especially remember be conscious of your comforting presence in the monotony of the day, and in the loneliness, and in the often sleepless nights. May the heart cry out, 'Your will be done!', and will you grant peace and restful slumber.

I pray your guidance on the diagnosis, and thank you for the dedication of all medical staff, and those who minister to the sick. I pray that the treatment given will relieve pain and distress, and if it be your will, result in a speedy recovery. I ask my prayers in the name of Jesus.

133

Dear God, I have come into your presence to pray for some people known to me who are unwell at this time. As I think of them, one by one, I will create a picture of them in my imagination. I will imagine them to be fit and healthy, because I believe that is your intention for them, as it is for everyone. Please accept every picture as a prayer:

I think of ....

I think of ....

I think of ....

Father, although I know that you want everyone to be physically, emotionally and spiritually whole, my experience of life tells me that this doesn't always come about. Sometimes this leaves me thinking that you are not as powerful as people say you are; but then I realise that thinking those kind of thoughts gets me nowhere. After all, the cross teaches me that your power is seen at its best in weakness.

My prayer for my friends is that your power will be demonstrated in their lives. If that means recovering full health, then I will praise you for it — and so will they. But if not, I pray that their weakness will still show your strength convincingly. May your power be shown through their peace, inner strength and serenity.

I make my prayers in the powerful name of Jesus.

Friends

134

Heavenly Father, I am so rich in my friends. I praise you for the abundant joy they have brought into my life.

I give thanks

for their lovely and varied personalities;
for the undemanding kindness they have shown me;
for the times when they have so readily supported me in
    trouble;
for their patience and cheerfulness.

I have been renewed by their strength,
    warmed by their love,
        encouraged by their praise,
            enabled to go on by their steadfast confidence in
            me.

Above all, I thank you for those precious moments when I have seen so clearly in them a reflection of you, so that my own love for you has been deepened and stirred.

Thank you, Lord, for the friends you have given me, and especially for ....

Help me, in return, to be a better friend, especially to those who feel alone and unwanted.

In your name I pray, my Friend of friends.

135

Thank you for friends,
Real friends who have loved
Over the years.
Friends that have never changed,
Never failed!
Gracious folk, spicing life,
Warming the heart,
Sharing without sparing;
Lovely folk, enriching life!

136

Life is so full of interest, Lord.

In all the shapes and shades of nature you have created infinite variety. Thank you, Lord!

Thank you for my family, Lord. There are differences of personality and interests in each of them, and I love them all . . . but I have some very special friends, too, Lord. And they are all so different! They add something to my personality. They accept me for what I am — an individual. They have no expectations of me. They do not demand loyalty, but I give it gladly.

They are my friends . . . and so too are you, Lord!

137

Sometimes, Lord, I need to justify my thoughts and actions. Too often I seem to fail to meet the goals others would see for me.

But I am encouraged, Lord. Encouraged when I remember that in your life on earth you were misunderstood. There were strong forces that challenged the way you spoke . . . that questioned your motives.

But there were exceptions. You had some close friends who accepted you; believed in you; loved you.

You needed their support, their loyalty. And you know that I need my friends for their love, their support, their loyalty.

Thank you, Lord, for each of them.

138

Thank you for my telephone, Lord!

So often I have complained that it is too intrusive. It takes up so much time, and is a distraction.

This morning, the 'phone call was from a friend.

Nothing important. Nothing urgent. Nothing demanded or expected of me. Just a call from a friend.

I need to keep in touch. Thank you for the telephone that brought an unexpected, cheering call from a friend. Help me, Lord, to remember to do the same — just call a friend on the 'phone, for no reason other than . . . well, to talk to a friend!

139

Loving heavenly Father, it is one of the greatest blessings of my life that I have this friendship with you. To come to you with open mind and heart, to be able to speak freely to you, to have no secrets from you, has created for me a sense of the truest friendship.

You will understand, then, the sadness I sometimes feel at the departure of dear friends who have stepped beyond the boundaries of this earthly life, and who have already met with you face to face. That I will never again on earth share their lively, joyous spirit brings a sense of grief; but how I rejoice to know that they are for ever safe in your tender care.

Because of all I have been given in friendship, I pray especially for all the friends who fill my life with joy, by bringing love, faithfulness, loyalty, understanding and wisdom. May they be aware today of your presence, and know that I am praying for them. Help me to let them know how much poorer my life would be without them, and without their friendship to light up the dark days. Their rich spirit has helped bring me closer to you.

You called your disciples friends, and shared with them all that the heavenly Father had made known to you. As you did with your disciples, so you do with me. Life would not be bearable without your friendship.

So, dear Lord, bless all those everywhere who give friendship unstintingly. Pour upon them the fullness of your grace. Shine your love into their hearts. I pray these blessings for all friends, and especially for those who are close and dear to me in friendship. Thank you for them.

140

'No man is an island', Lord. The poet of long ago taught us this, yet how slow we are to learn. We confess that too often we fail to see the way in which our actions, our words, our attitudes will affect others. I have been just as guilty as anyone else, Lord.

I pray just now, Father, for this community in which I live, that it shall be a community in which each is aware of the other's needs, abilities, weaknesses and aspirations.

I pray for the community which is my home; may all who go out from it represent Christ in their daily tasks.

I pray for the community which is my neighbourhood; may all be blessed with a sense of caring and sharing, of encouraging and supporting.

I pray for the community which is the political district in which I live; may its representatives become aware of the potential which is amongst its people — not only potential for votes, but for contributing to the strength of the nation. May those leaders be sensitive also to every need.

I pray for the community which is my nation; I thank you for its proud history, and for its present strengths. I rejoice in its qualities, and I share in repenting for its sins of selfishness and pride and greed. Lord, bless our land and its peoples; let us see that we are most honoured when we honour you. In seeking good for ourselves, let us ever be mindful of the needs of all your children, whether within our own shores, or far away.

And I pray, Lord, for the community of nations; I can do little more than bring before you national leaders and international leaders — leaders in a world that is weary with war, and hunger, and homelessness and strife of many kinds. I add my small voice to those others in praying, 'Peace — in *our* time, O Lord'.

141

O Lord, you fashioned us to live at peace with each other in small communities, and made of us a great nation. It was your will that we should build each other up in love and righteousness, bringing honour and glory to your name. I mourn that we have fallen from that great ideal. We have lost sight of you as we have followed selfish ends.

Lord, through your Spirit, challenge our community and nation. Let us catch the vision of what we could become if we but looked to you and obeyed you.

Whatever I can do or be to help this prayer become reality, do but make clear to me, and your will shall be done.

In Jesus' name and for his sake.

142

Sovereign Lord of the nations, you rule over all peoples with love and justice.

I look in vain for evidence that we are learning to live together in harmony as one world. There are pockets of resistance to peace in every nation.

I recognise that they exist within my own heart, as well.

Forgive my preoccupation with self, and centre my heart upon Jesus the Christ, to whom all true authority is given.

143

Almighty and eternal God, this community in which you have placed me is so diverse I hardly know where to begin in prayer.

Our clothing styles separate us; our languages shout out our differences; and our rush to get about our business keeps our eyes on the pavement and not on each other.

Lord, I'm part of the problem, as well. My prejudices are real, and my suspicions are a factor needing your corrective focus.

As you reconciled me through Christ, so make me a reconciling agent for change in this community.

144

Gracious God, that man looked at me with such suspicion!
He made me feel like an alien!
My innocent gesture
caused him to recoil
as if wounded.
Yet skin is skin, no matter what the colour;
blood is red, no matter who bleeds.
Help me try again
next time.

145

Lord, behind all these closed doors, as I walk around this neighbourhood, are lives I know nothing about. I may get the occasional glimpse through an expression on someone's face, or a word of greeting. I may read about folk in the local newspaper. But I can truly know so few.

May the few lives that I can connect with, in turn connect with others, so that the people of this neighbourhood – unknown to me – will know themselves to be known to you.

The wider world

146

My heart is saddened, Lord, for I have just heard the news of the latest tragedy. People have died, others have been hurt, there has been damage and destruction.

Sometimes it is an extreme of nature which causes such horror and distress; sometimes it is a genuine accident, or an act of carelessness on someone's part; sometimes it is the result of greed and bitterness and hatred.

My concern in prayer, Lord, is for people who are involved. The people who just now are agonising in great pain; those who have been bereaved as a result of the tragedy; those who are in a state of shock and bewilderment; those who may be homeless; those who in any way feel themselves to have been responsible, and who are finding it so hard to live with themselves. To all of these, Lord, and to any others who have been touched in some way by this latest event, come with your calming and healing grace.

Give strength and wisdom to those who go with succour to the place of need. I thank you that there always are such people, bringing commitment and so many skills into a tragic situation. May their service be offered to your children, as though it were being offered to you. And may Jesus himself be in the midst.

147

Father, who knows better than you that by nature I'm an insecure person. I feel safest in my own little world, and prefer to stay in it! My real interests tend to be limited to *my* family, *my* job, *my* money, *my* health and *my* future. I sometimes think about my soul, but that's only right, isn't it?

I have a sneaking suspicion that my problem could have more to do with selfishness than insecurity.

Help me, please, to tear down my walls. There's another world out there for which you have made me responsible. Make me *feel* responsible. Make me *care*. It's a suffering world, and I should be doing something about it.

Push me, please!

148

Lord
When will it end?
— the killing
— the hunger
— the wars
Our inhumanity to each other!

Lord
When will it end?
— the abuse
— the exploitation
— the rejection
Our insensitivity to each other!

Lord
When will it end?
— the arrogance
— the anger
— the uncertainty
Our impatience to each other!

The world is small, we see too much;
O God, who came the aching heart to touch,
If you can still the wild and raging sea,
Then you can calm the fears inside of me.

149

Dear God and Father of all, I look at the many blessings
with which you have surrounded me, and my heart truly
overflows with thanksgiving and rejoicing. I say with the
psalmist, 'Who am I, that you should be so mindful of

me?' Because of your goodness and love toward me, I realise my need to reach out to the world — my community, my city, my country — and bring to you in prayer those who are outside of your family. Stir in my heart a deep and true concern for those who yet walk in darkness, and have no knowledge of your light, your love and your salvation.

Make me more aware of the needs of the poor and the homeless, the drug addicts and the desperately ill, all those who are helpless because no one tells them to turn to you for help. How little I truly know, Lord, of all they face day after day. For your sake, I long for their redemption, and ask that I may do whatever I can to ease their burdens.

I pray for our country. How much it stands in need of your leadership and guidance. Direct our leaders, and all those in authority. May they put aside personal ambition and put the welfare of the people first in all their endeavours. May they understand that they will only truly succeed if they seek to follow your leadings.

Remind me continually, Lord, that with you there is nothing impossible, and that prayer can and does change things. Let it be so, dear Father, I pray in Jesus' name.

150

Dear God, hardly a day goes by without we hear words like,

'fighting has broken out . . .'

or

'a bomb has exploded in a crowded store . . .'

or

'another soldier was shot dead today. . .'

. . . and it depresses me, Father, it really depresses me. Why does there have to be so much hatred and anger in the world? Why are we so obsessed with retaliation and revenge? Why do we have to behave as if we had never heard of peace? Why? Why? Why?

I think I'm beginning to discover the answer, Father. It's because we've forgotten what love means. No one wants to destroy what he loves — that's madness! It's impossible! Love can't hurt or harm. Love wants only to help and heal.

Father, I long for peace. I want peace in my home — peace in my country — peace in the world. Can these prayers be answered?

Yes, Father! Thank you for showing me that every time I ask for peace, I should really be asking for love. And if I ask for love, you will give me peace.

Somehow, it's harder to pray for love, Father, but I know you are right. You always are. So help me to love. . . .

Please!

151

I worship you as Lord over all. The peoples and nations are yours. Your love embraces the whole of the earth —

the earth with its beauty and its ugliness; its agonies and its delights; its infinite diversity of peoples and cultures; its common human story of hope and despair, of sin and grace, of abundance and need, of violence and gentle acts of healing. It is all yours. You so loved this world that you gave your Son to be its Saviour. In his coming to us, you bonded yourself with us, taking our identity, our history of inhumanity and of indifference to the poverty and pain and powerlessness of our sisters and brothers around the world.

I confess that I do not like the ugliness of the world to intrude upon my comfortable and well-ordered life. I have enough to deal with at home. I want to close my eyes and ears to the hungry and oppressed. But you call me to listen — to feel their anger and frustration. You call me to look — as Jesus looked on the crowds, milling about as sheep without a shepherd. You call me insistently to reach out and touch the agonies of the world with compassion. Help me to see what small steps I might take toward responsible living in such a world.

I pray for those who are at risk in the areas of the world that are most troubled. Provide for their needs out of your rich store. Grant them a sense of your presence with them. Help them to know that even when they are most frustrated about their needs, they can be symbols of hope and standard-bearers of the Kingdom of God.

I pray for those who walk in darkness and the shadow of death, on whom the light has yet to shine. Inflame and empower all those who are bearers of the light to them. Sustain them in their witness. Keep them patient and hopeful. Grant them the joy of seeing your grace irradiate the lives of those about them.

Give courage to those who live where there is fear of reprisal and persecution because of their faith in Christ. Grant them boldness.

Give grace to every agency that seeks to project the light of the gospel into the night that surrounds them. And set your people free, through Jesus, 'the sacrifice . . . for the sins of the whole world'.

Stretch my faith to encompass the world you love, and for which Christ lived and died and is alive for evermore. In his name.

The homeless

152

O loving Lord Jesus Christ, I want to share in prayer with you today the burden we hear so much about — that of homelessness.

Lord, you have blessed me with so much. As I talk with you like this, life's problems surround me. Today, as usual, I have had more than sufficient food to eat, whilst the homeless often look in vain for something to satisfy their hunger. Lord, meet their need.

From the peace and safety of my home, where I find so much acceptance and love, I think of and pray for those who have none of these benefits and blessings. Lord, meet their need.

Tonight, I will rest in a warm and comfortable bed, and I thank you for such a blessing as this. Please undertake for those who sleep rough, or wander the streets with nowhere to rest. Then, Lord, I recall that you had nowhere to lay your head, and that you know far better than I do what it is really like. By choice, Lord Jesus, you became homeless and experienced rejection, so that you would always and forever understand when people lose their homes. So be pleased to bless such needy people, and open the hearts of all of us who are favoured with material blessings to do something to help them.

In your name I pray.

153

O Lord, what a joy it is to come home at the end of a long day, to the love and warmth of my family: to a hot meal; to an evening of peace and relaxation; to a time of enjoying television or sitting quietly by the fireside; to a book or the fellowship of conversation. As the day ends, I bid good-night to loved ones, and climb into my warm, comfortable bed. Thank you, Lord, for my home.

But, Lord, when I am safely cuddled up, there are so many out there still walking the streets, tired, hungry, cold. They beg for food, they have no place to relax, they have no one with whom to share the news of the day. As the evening comes to its end, there is no one to say goodnight. They are alone. Some will curl up in doorways; others will take refuge in cardboard boxes; some will find a park bench for a bed and a newspaper for a blanket. Lord, they have no place to call home.

Lord, it's not enough for me to say I care. The reality of the way they live is so grim that it rips through my heart like a knife. I cannot deny it; I cannot close my eyes to it. Our world, my world, has so many of those we call 'the homeless'. Lord, show me how I can make the world a better place for them.

Who will bid the homeless good morning? What will they eat for breakfast or will the pangs of hunger remain theirs as they pass by the cafes? Lord, help me to see the need, but also help me to meet it.

I am only one person, Lord, and the homeless are so many. I can't help them all. But you can, Lord. As you fed the five thousand with a few loaves and fishes, will you feed the hungry with the abundance which is all around us, and so poorly used. Motivate me to do what I can do, and to put what I am and what I have into your hands — for their sakes.

154

Father God, I thank you for every comfort with which you so graciously provide me. Not least amongst my blessings are those of home and family and friends. Yet my joy is lessened as my thoughts turn toward those who have neither home nor family nor close friends. How tragic is their situation as they lay down, night after night, in the open, whatever the weather may be. How sad is their plight, aimlessly wandering the streets by day, with no one seemingly to care for them.

Grant that they may be aware that they matter to you, and that you care for them deeply. May they know of your heart reaching out in compassion to them. May your love be revealed to them through those who in the name of Christ Jesus seek to make practical provision to meet their many needs.

Give guidance to government in making adequate provision for the homeless. Sanctify the ministry of all agencies and individuals who aid them in their distress. Show me, Lord, if there is any practical action in which I should be involved on their behalf, no matter how costly to me it may be.

All this I ask, remembering your compassion and works in meeting human needs.

155

O God of all compassion, look down I pray upon the homeless who wander the streets by day and night. How vulnerable they are — especially the young people — to those who would exploit them for unseemly ends. Protect them from such, I pray. Grant that through your grace they might find courage and the means to reorganise their lives in constructive ways. Guide them to people who really care, who are committed, and who have the skills to help them in the ways they so much need. This I ask in the name of Jesus, in whom is the hope of newness of life for them, and for us all.

156

Dear Lord Jesus, praying for the homeless is not easy, because I am praying to you from within a safe and happy home. You have no favourite children, yet I have never for one night been homeless, and my heart is heavy when I consider the deprivation of others.

I pray on behalf of all who are refugees; those people who are owned by no country, and who are dispossessed; people who have had to seek political asylum, leaving loved ones behind; others who have entered countries illegally, and who are living in fear of deportation; immigrants who feel alien as they battle with a new language and new culture in a strange land. Please give your guidance to all who try to help them, including politicians and lawyers.

I pray for those whose homes have been destroyed by merciless violence in war-torn countries; people from ordinary homes, senselessly bombed or set on fire. Please bless all who serve with peace-keeping forces, and all those others — well-known and unknown — who seek to be peacemakers.

I pray for the homeless victims of famine; those who, in spite of weakness, must travel great distances to escape aggressors or to find food. The sick die, and children cry for sustenance which parents cannot give. I pray for all who administer food aid, for reporters in the media, for the drivers of lorries and for aircrew seeking to deliver food, in spite of danger. I pray, too, for staff of all voluntary agencies at work on behalf of famine ridden countries.

I pray for those who have lost their homes through disasters such as floods, fires, storms and major accidents. Let there be friends and helpers to support them, and please work through the responses of welfare agencies and governments.

I pray, Lord, for those children I see on television, who live in primitive mental hospitals, and under-resourced children's homes, where even basic needs cannot be met.

When I consider such great needs, it would be so easy to feel helplessly overwhelmed. But you, Lord Jesus, are the Saviour of the world, and its hope. Your heart is moved by compassion for every one of your suffering and needy children, and your Spirit is constantly at work to help them. Thank you, Lord.

157

Dear Lord Jesus, I pray for those in my own country who are homeless.

I pray for families caught up in escalating debt, who cannot pay their rent, and have had to leave their homes. Please help all who seek to relieve their poverty, and stop their downward social spiral.

I pray for street children; children abandoned by parents who do not want them, or cannot maintain them; children who have run away from heedless parents, or who have felt unwanted when a parent found a new partner.

I pray for those who sleep on pavements because they suffer from mental illness, or the ravages of addiction. Please help me at least to smile at them as I pass. Bless all outreach and street workers, the staff of day centres, and also officials in social welfare and housing departments.

I pray for any who will be released from prison, and who will have no place of welcome. Their knock on the door of relatives may cause only fear, and a hope that they might go away. Sadly, Lord, I confess that I would not really want them to come and live in my block of flats, either. I pray for the work of prison reformers, prison chaplains and probation officers.

I pray for all who live within houses which are not homes, because they are places without love or laughter, peace or solace. I especially pray for children torn apart by their parents' strife-ridden relationship, or who live in fear of cruel or abusing parents. Please bless all who work to safeguard children in such surroundings.

I thank you for the great privilege of being a co-worker with you. Help me to be obedient to every impulse that you give me to help others. I know that by every prayer, every deed of kindness, every act of justice or selfless love your Kingdom comes to the world for which you died.

The hungry

158

Father, my immediate response is to turn away when I see yet another news report of people who are literally starving to death in what we so glibly call 'the third world'. I prefer not to look at the bloated stomachs of little children, the desperate eyes of emaciated mothers whose milk has gone because they themselves are undernourished, the hunched postures of older men which reflect their sense of hopelessness.

Forgive me, Father, for when I force myself to look I realise afresh that there is no such thing as the third world — or for that matter a first or second world. This world is your world, and every person in it is your child. How can I say I love you when I prefer to blot from my mind the disconcerting picture of my brothers and sisters who suffer so terribly? Help me, rather, to dare in some small way to enter into your feelings as you view their plight, knowing that you have made ample provision for your children, but knowing also that selfishness and greed have resulted in an unfair distribution of the resources you have so freely given.

May I reflect the constancy of your love for your children in the consistency of my concern for them. Show me how I can translate that concern into my approach to everyday living. May my own daily hungering and thirsting for righteousness reveal itself in:

> good stewardship of the food resources I enjoy;
> a deeply thankful heart for every meal I eat;

prayerful response to opportunities to give monetary support — to those who bring short-term emergency relief to the hungry; or to those who seek to help them to longer-term solutions, by educating them in how to maximise their meagre resources.

Above all, strengthen my belief in the promise that there will be a day when righteousness will prevail, and when all who long for it will be completely satisfied.

In the name of Jesus Christ I pray.

159

O Bread of Life, I bring to you those whose bellies have never known a decent meal. I lay before you children who cry themselves to sleep with hunger, and parents who despair as they see their families slowly starve. I know, Lord Jesus, that there is enough food in the world to feed everyone, and I implore you to open the selfish hearts of those who hoard food and profiteer out of human misery. Dear Christ, should they be allowed to feel just a breath of Hell, so they might be moved to compassion?

My Saviour, help me to do my part personally to share with the hungry — not only the food which will satisfy their bodies, but also to share you, the true bread of life. For you will satisfy them eternally.

In your name I pray.

160

O Lord, whose human hands were quick
To feed the hungry, heal the sick,
Who love by loving deed expressed,
Help me to comfort the distressed.

What is divine about my creed
If I am blind to human need?
For you have said they serve you best
Who serve the helpless and oppressed.

Lord may your love translucent shine
Through every loving deed of mine,
That men may see the works I do
And give the glory all to you.

161

Heavenly Father, you have always carried the oppressed, forgotten and rejected on your heart. Down through the generations you have loved them, and sought to kindle love within your people for them. We have been slow to learn. *I* have been slow to learn. Even though our Lord Jesus taught us that when we love and serve them we are loving and serving him, we still allow their needs to be obscured and unmet. The burden they represent is too heavy, Lord, for me to carry. Help me, therefore, to understand that as part of Christ's body on earth, there is a positive work that can be done for them. They do not have to remain oppressed and deprived. Increase my awareness, that I may pray more for them, give more for them and, when the opportunity comes, do more for them — because they belong to you and are precious to you.

I ask in Jesus' name.

162

Father in Heaven, we ask
Bless those who suffer,
Imprisoned, impoverished, impounded
For righteousness' sake.
Day after day they suffer in silence,
Tormented in mind,
Whilst loved ones wait,
Fearing, hoping, praying.
Deliverance we ask;
In you alone is hope,
And so we pray on,
Believing, trusting, confident
In divine intervention.

163

I thank you, O Father, for all those people in our society who undertake the care of the needy. When their work seems too demanding and unrewarding, give them new strength.

I pray that all such service will be offered in the spirit of the one who declared, 'I came not to be ministered unto, but to minister'.

164

Father God, you remember, accept and empower your own. But there are those who, although your children, remain oppressed, forgotten, rejected by the world.

Some are oppressed by power-mongers, victims of those with voracious appetites. But you know them.

Others are forgotten as they become nameless faces in the crowd, those who struggle simply to sustain themselves with the essentials of life. Such are the elderly, the morally, physically and mentally weak, the compliant, all who lack the voice to make themselves known. But you know them.

There are still others who are rejected. Because of deformity or abnormality, they do not make the grade in a world where might is right. But you know them.

Remember, accept and empower those of your children who are an echo of your own hours of oppression and rejection.

Because you have overcome the world, we claim your care for all the oppressed, forgotten and rejected. May we who have been remembered, accepted and empowered by you be the means of consolation through the grace which you have placed within us.

165

Lord, I have never really been hungry in the way that some of my fellow human beings have. I have never really been without shelter, or known the pain of hurtful rejection. I have not been oppressed by the persecution of a conqueror, nor sensed that I have been really overlooked or forgotten.

I offer, dear Lord, my grateful thanks for every mercy — realised or blindly accepted. I lift my heart in prayer for those who have suffered . . . who still suffer . . . and who will suffer the denial of basic human rights, and be brought into a situation of extreme need.

Lord, where the problem is that of distribution, of fair dealing, or lack of awareness by the self-satisfied, please help those who are more fortunate to give and to share more equably.

May your Spirit continue to strive in men's hearts, until as many as possible are satisfied, and their needs assuaged. In Jesus' name I pray.

The churches and their ministry

166

O God, I pray for all those who have the responsibility to proclaim the truth which you have revealed to them. Grant that they may speak with clarity, that they may make your word relevant to those who hear, and that they may be always faithful to their task. May the response of those who receive the word be an encouragement to your ministers.

I ask that you will especially bless those men and women who have been called to positions of authority in your Church. May your Holy Spirit so direct and empower them that they may develop qualities of spirituality, character and leadership. Whatever the nature of their responsibilities may be, help them to be effective in their teaching and administration so that your people may be encouraged and established in the faith.

167

I have a burden on my heart, Lord, that the churches and those in the ministry of the gospel shall be totally committed to your will and to the direction of the Holy Spirit.

I plead for the faithfulness of church members as they meet together week by week, that they may truly reach out to attain the qualities which are God-given, and which attract the unsaved to you. May they seek to honour you in all they say, and may you be glorified in every activity in which they engage.

For those who minister, I ask that they will know and feel a sense of security which comes when the Holy Spirit dwells within. May they be filled with a spontaneous joy from above, which reaches out to our sad world, and brightens the lives of those with whom they come into contact. May they have peace which will calm the distressed and soothe the sorrowing. May they have wisdom which will open many doors, and allow the light of understanding to fill the church with its splendour, as you reveal yourself to their congregations through their ministry. For Jesus' sake.

The nation's leaders

168

Almighty God, today I pray for our nation's leaders. I acknowledge that their responsibilities are great, and that their decisions will not meet with everyone's approval.

As they seek to govern, may they remember the example of Jesus who, though greater than any man, made himself of 'no reputation' as he made the concern of others his first priority.

May the humility, faithfulness and obedience of Jesus be an inspiration and challenge to those entrusted with the care of the nation's welfare.

I pray that you will give to those who ask the wisdom to govern justly, the patience not to seek easy and quick and expedient solutions, and the courage always to do what is right.

As our leaders seek to maintain or forge new relationships with leaders of other nations, may they hold those others in respect, remembering that you are the Father of all mankind, who loves each nation equally.

169

Father God, how privileged I am to place before you in the privacy of this room, the needs of the nation's leaders, some of whom are Christians, some of other faiths, and others indifferent to any revelation of yourself in the world.

I long for the time when 'at the name of Jesus every knee shall bow', but I now centre my thoughts upon present-day leaders in response to the apostle Paul's urging to pray for those in authority.

Guide those who by their conduct and status greatly influence the moral and spiritual climate of this land, and awaken the conscience of those who, either deliberately or unintentionally, undermine Christian values and standards. Especially do I pray that Christian leaders will speak and act in a manner that will personify your commandments and Christ's teachings.

Grant to the leaders of every governing body, and to all who have responsibility for administering the laws of the land, a desire to further the good of the nation above their personal ambitions and political differences.

I pray for commercial and industrial stability; for increasing understanding between the captains of industry and trade union leaders, that they may be sensitive to each other's points of view, knowing that upon their judgments and decisions depend the welfare of ordinary men and women.

For leaders in the field of education, I ask that there might be a recognition of the needs of the whole person in the implementation of educational programmes, so that every individual is given opportunity to reach full potential.

O God, your Son Jesus Christ was spoken of by the prophet Isaiah as leader and commander. Hasten the day when leaders in all walks of life shall follow the example he has set and the precepts he has given, subscribing to the truth that 'righteousness exalts a nation'.

PART II

PRAYERS FOR PUBLIC USE

SUNDAY WORSHIP AND MIDWEEK MEETINGS

Sunday morning worship

170

(Call to worship)

This, then, is *the Lord's day*,
No arid Sabbath here, with overtones of duty;
But worship steeped with Resurrection joy —
An indication and a promise of new life.

We, then, are *the Lord's people* —
Not all of us committed;
But each of us love-touched with thoughts of Christ,
And God the Father, and the Holy Spirit.

So — *day and people* come together
With longing, adoration; and with hope
That out of this sweet union
Shall be born new faith, new strength!

171

O God, our eternal Father, in the name of Jesus and through the Holy Spirit, we come into your presence this morning.

We have come with several intentions and many hopes. As we spend our time here, may we give right priorities both to our intentions and our hopes, so that we shall depart richer in spirit than when we arrived.

We come first of all with our worship, adoring you as Creator, Preserver and Governor of all things. May we in our hearts, as well as with our lips, acknowledge you as rightful Lord of our lives. May we know what it means to enthrone you as King. May we also see you setting aside your majesty to become man amongst men. As we learn truly to worship you, O God, so then will all our other relationships with you be hallowed and sanctified by that worship.

We acknowledge you as Lord and King, and we praise you — not only for who you are, but also for what you have done and are doing amongst your people. We have fallen far short of your desires for us, yet you continually give us blessings, and allow us further opportunities of growing in grace. We thank you, our Father, for Jesus, whose life, death and resurrection provided both the pattern and the power for holy living. May we realise his presence among us.

We meet in his name, and pray that as a result of being in this place today our lives will be enriched for the Kingdom's sake, and not just for our own blessing; teach us that worship must always place you and your will at the centre of our attention.

We bring before you, O God, those of this congregation who are unable or even unwilling to meet with us in fellowship. We covet them and pray that where they are you will speak to them in love through our intercessions.

Our prayer reaches out beyond these walls to those many others for whom our prayers and practical concern are so important. Help us to keep faith with them — the poor, the sick, the hopeless and helpless and inadequate. Let us be as Christ in the world to them. Let us most of all be constant in our aspirations for those who have not yet seen your love in the redeeming sacrifice of Jesus.

May our offering of music, the spoken word, and our uplifted hearts be acceptable to you, and may your name be glorified. As we leave this place, we pray that we shall do so refreshed in mind, restored in spirit, and renewed in hope. Through Jesus Christ our Lord.

172

Almighty God, we reflect on the week now past, with its responsibilities and its busyness. May the labours of our hands, the thoughts of our minds and the inclinations of our hearts have been to our credit and not to our discredit, and all to your honour.

Many of us have needed to get by on a minimum of prayer, so great have been the demands upon our time. The spirit of devotion to Christ our Lord has not been easy to maintain.

But now, Lord, we hear the morning call to worship — the 'sweet hour of prayer'. We come to drink deeply of the wells of salvation. 'Holy, holy, holy, Lord God Almighty! Early in the morning our song shall rise to thee'.

We enclose also within our circle of prayer those whose lives touch our own — business colleague, neighbour, friend, family, including the little ones. We remember especially the elderly and frail, for whom life sometimes seems such a burden.

We pray in the sure confidence that 'if with all our hearts we seek you, we shall ever surely find you', who are God in three Persons, blessed Trinity.

173

O Lord our God, we pray for your blessing upon the worship and the work of our congregation

— that we may be a praying people

— that our building may be a centre of Christian truth

— that service in the community may be an increasing joy

— that each of us may be a witness to your redeeming love,

through Jesus Christ our Lord.

174

We give thanks, Lord, for the call to prayer and praise, grateful for the open door to worship. Our needy hearts have learned to lean with confidence on all this hour will hold. Our thirsty spirits will again drink deeply of the water of life which flows here. Accept us, and bless us with your healing and renewing presence.

We come, Lord, to give thanks for all of life's blessings, for the busy round of work and home; for the provision also of rest and holidays. We think prayerfully of our children, and of the truths which they learn in this place.

We ask that good success may attend the work of all who minister to our young people.

We come, Lord, with confidence in the gospel. Our hearts have learned to exclaim, 'Lord, to whom else can we go? Thou hast the words of eternal life.' Keep us closely in your fellowship, glad to be numbered in the company of those who believe and trust in you.

And as we so pray, we remember also some who do not find it easy to walk in your way. We pass no judgment upon them, but trust that, as our love goes out to them just now, so your love will not leave them untouched and unenlightened.

We pray through Jesus Christ our Lord, whose name we honour, in whose love we trust, and of whose Kingdom we are citizens.

175

O God, our almighty Father, we thank you for the week which is past, for day succeeding day, for all that has been asked of us, and for all that has been gifted to us. We reflect on our working hours, and offer to you all the labour of mind and hand, whether in the home or at our place of employment. We reflect upon our leisure hours, and thank you for ease of mind and body — not least for the blessing of sleep and the provision of holidays. We reflect on the lessons we have learned in study, from the newspapers, from radio and television. We prayerfully reflect on every experience, on the decisions made, the choices accepted, the friendships strengthened, and on every endeavour to follow Christ in all things.

In this house of faith, on the first day of the week, we thank you for the opportunity for prayer and praise. Help us to profit from the mistakes of the past, and to do well that which we have done indifferently. Help us to be kind where we would be impatient, and to grow more nearly to the image of Christ as we perceive him.

With all these thoughts in mind, we open our spirits to the light and the truth of your Holy Spirit, who is with us, among us and within us.

176

Dear Lord, we come before you to worship, not to forget the cares of the world, nor leave them outside the door. We bring them before you to cradle, whilst we bathe in the beauty of your presence, freed to respond to your call.

Speak to our hearts that are hungry, helping us explore the depths of your love. Strengthen our passion, with understanding and the will to reach others as extensions of your arms of love.

177

We thank you, Lord, for your love, which makes it possible for us to love one another.

We thank you for the privilege of gathering in this hallowed place, to hear your word, and to praise your name.

We have come to be filled with the bread of life, and to be inspired by your Holy Spirit.

Now, Lord, meet every need, mend every broken spirit, challenge every heart and mind with your life-giving word. And make us worthy of the name of Christian. For Jesus' sake.

178

Dear Father, we thank you for the gift of this new day, and for the privileged opportunity which is ours of gathering in your presence. We have come into this place having had so many different experiences during this past week: times of joy and times of sorrow, times of victory and times of failure. Not one of us comes before you untainted, unscathed, unaffected, untouched by those things which offend you. At the very beginning of our time together, therefore, we confess our sin to you.

As we look back at days past, we see those things which we ought not to have done; we see, too, those things which we should have done, but failed to do. There are words that we should not have allowed to slip out; and there are other words that we ought to have said, but which were left unuttered. We thought we had our reasons; we justified ourselves; we compared ourselves with others who also claim to love you, and who do as we did. But in the light of Jesus, we know that we have no defence. We allowed our own concerns, our own feelings, our own fears to control us, rather than his Spirit of holiness.

Dear Father, forgive those attitudes, revealed in what we say and what we do, which are not of the Spirit of Christ. In these moments of silence, as each of us allows you to reveal particular weaknesses that have grieved you, may we offer them to you for cleansing, with a desire not to hurt you or your Kingdom or each other again. May we know your forgiveness as you create a new and right spirit within us.

May anything about us which gets in the way of your will for us be removed. Empty us of all that is not of you, that you might fill us with yourself, the Holy Spirit.

179

Our Father God, once more we come to you in worship. We want to praise you, to express our love to you, and to thank you that your Son, our dear Lord Jesus Christ, opened wide his arms for us on the cross, saving us from the consequences of our sin, and setting us free to serve you as your holy people.

Not all of us feel able to praise you this morning. Some are in dread of the week to come, some are very worried and tense and mentally exhausted, and some are living lives of quiet desperation. Whatever our circumstances, help us all to hold on to the fact that you know, understand and care about what is happening to us. Give us this confidence even when we cannot feel or see your presence in our lives. Grant us, we pray, the courage to keep going, and the maturity to realise that there is hope — and that we must share our Lord's sufferings if we are to share his glory.

Almighty God, many of your early saints frequently prayed in such a manner and to such effect that they were perceived to be 'pulling the glory down'. Times change, and approaches change, but the desire of our hearts in this meeting is identical to theirs of old.

We pray that your Holy Spirit shall so fill us, whether in a spectacular way or in a quieter way, that we might worship you as you would be worshipped, and serve you with holy and effective lives.

Whatever our role in this act of worship, help us to relax, to concentrate and to learn. Above all, may your Holy Spirit empower all that is said and done, so that we may each one be more fitted for service.

All these things we ask for your greater glory.

180

Heavenly Father, we thank you for the gift of this day, which allows us to come together to worship, to celebrate, to discover truth and to find new inner strength.

We worship you: in the quietness we meditate on your power, your might, your holiness, and your love, and we give you the glory due to your name. We adore you, we praise you, we thank you, we love you.

We come together today to celebrate. We celebrate the resurrection of our Lord Jesus Christ, and the reality of his living presence among us. We celebrate the miracle of the Church, the body of Christ, and we thank you that we belong to it. We celebrate the distinctive fellowship of those who belong to Christ, and praise you for what that means to us here in our own special place of worship.

We want to discover new truth today. Some of us may feel that our minds and bodies are tired after a demanding week, but our hearts are hungry for new insights into your nature and your will. We ask that your Holy Spirit will lead us into truth as we seek after it.

And we come confessing our needs. We need forgiveness for our sins; we need guidance in our confusion; we need strength for our feelings of weakness; we need peace to ease our stress. We ask that our needs may be met here today as we open our hearts to receive your love, so clearly revealed in Jesus.

We pray for this act of worship. Please guide and direct whoever shall lead us and minister your holy word.

We make our prayers in the name of Jesus, our living Lord.

181

Dear Father God, it is so good to be in your house this morning, so good to be able to worship and praise you in music and song. As we read your word, and consider the works of your hands, we are warmed in our hearts and uplifted in our spirits.

We thank you for the blessings of corporate worship, for the good feelings and sense of fellowship we experience as we come together like this.

At this point in our worship, we come to you for ourselves individually. Lord, we acknowledge our great need of you in our lives, and we quieten our hearts and our minds in preparation for what you have to say to us. We ask you to be present with us . . . as we concentrate upon you . . . as we bring our needs to you.

God, you know and understand the stresses, tensions and complexities in our daily lives. We bring them to you now. Help us not to give in to the fears and anxieties that grip us. Be with us as we pray, as we trust, as we lean upon you.

Forgive us, Lord, for our wilful and wayward actions, for the times we allow ourselves to be controlled by mixed motives, and distracted by false goals. Be with us as we pray, as we trust, as we lean upon you.

Lord, we come to you knowing that alone we cannot correct our basic sinful nature. We ask you to cleanse and renew and restore us. We yearn for the transforming power of your Holy Spirit in our lives. Create in each of us a pure heart, and renew a steadfast spirit within us. Grant us willing hearts to do your will, and above all fill us with the joy of your Holy Spirit.

O God, hear our earnest prayers as we further wait upon you.

182

(Confession)

O Lord, on this Sunday morning, help us to still our hearts and minds in your presence, and to seek fellowship with you. Help us to understand, amid all the faltering steps we take, that our ultimate aspiration must be to seek your Kingdom and your righteousness.

We confess this morning, O Lord, that all too often we have sought counterfeit kingdoms which have turned to ashes. We have, all too often, been satisfied with our own self-righteousness and pride. Forgive us, Lord, for our contentment with the things that have supplanted you, and that are unworthy of you, and unworthy of our devotion.

See us this morning, Father, as children of the King, wayward and wandering at times, but still your children, with love pouring out from broken and contrite hearts, for this we know you will never despise.

Take not your Holy Spirit from us; cast us not away from your presence, but create within us, O Lord, clean hearts. Restore to us lost joys, and the strength of your Spirit. We acknowledge our transgressions, and our sin is ever before us. Have mercy upon us, O Lord, according to your great and immeasurable love and mercy.

Father God, hear our prayer this morning, made to you in the namc of Jesus, our precious Redeemer.

183

Dear Heavenly Father,
on this day ordained

for rest and worship,
we come to you,
confident of your love
and of your desire to give
us your best and highest gifts.

We bring to you this hour
   the deepest longings of our souls,
   the thirst that no earthly springs can quench,
   the hunger that no earthly bread can satisfy,
   the needs that the world cannot meet.
Sanctify our imagination
   with a vision of the new heights
   of holiness you have for us.
Save us from mediocrity.
Deliver us from lesser things
   that would incapacitate our spirits.
Make us willing to be changed.

We pray that you will give us:
   power for our weakness,
   wisdom for our guidance,
   peace for our anxieties,
   healing for our hurts,
   cleansing for our sin,
   your holiness for our living.

Unite us this hour
   in a fellowship of discovery.
Nourish our minds with your truth.
Overflow our hearts with your love.
Explode in us new possibilities
   for holy living and sanctified service
   through the gracious ministry
   of your Holy Spirit.

184

Dear Lord, we come consciously and carefully into your presence in this evening hour, trusting that you have already made your dwelling here.

We have come to worship and to pray; we wish to see Jesus, and to be blessed by him. We long to be refreshed again within our hearts with that love which made possible our salvation; that love which attracts men and women of the world to gather in fellowship — to sing and to pray and to speak and to praise.

Almighty God, through our singing and our witness, and through the ministry of the holy Scriptures, let us once more be reminded that our Lord Jesus Christ has, by his suffering and death, made an atonement for the whole world, so that whoever believes in him might have salvation. Whether long on the Christian pilgrimage, or not yet started, may each of us in this place have a vision of a way to eternal life, opened by the teaching, the living, the dying and the resurrection of our Lord.

May the prayers of intercession which rise from this congregation be acceptable to you, our Father, and may many be blessed in body and soul as we pray for them in the name of Jesus. Let us not be selfish in our praying; we have been so much enriched in so many ways by your love, and now we covet those same blessings, and more, for the whole world.

As we now wait on you in faith, we pray that our hearts shall be open to receive truth. And as we receive, O God, we ask that we shall not be hearers of the word only, but that our lives will hereafter show forth those things that your love has made known.

In the name of Jesus Christ we pray.

185

Dear Father God, so often we come to you to receive — yet is there a moment in any day when we are not already receiving your love, your mercy, your provision, your listening ear?

May our gathering here this evening, Lord, be expressly to give: to give honour and glory and worship to you, and to give ourselves in the building up and the edifying of one another. Rather than meeting here only to receive blessing, may our deepest desire be to impart blessing. We know that you are no man's debtor, and that you will not allow us to leave this place without being enriched, if we ourselves have sought to be channels of your grace to others.

We pray for and covet those who belong to our fellowship, but who are absent. Especially would we pray for the sick and the housebound; for faithful fellow-worshippers whose hearts are with us, even though they cannot be physically present. At this moment, by your Holy Spirit's power, and in the mysterious way that only you can, make them aware of our prayers and your love. May we all feel your healing touch, and have an experience of physical, mental and spiritual restoration.

In our community, there are others who once joined with us, those who were once part of our household of faith, and who had a great love and desire for you. Lord, speak to them, and let our own actions on their behalf reveal that our prayers are more than just empty words. May we have a longing for the lost that will not be satisfied until they know the joy of a restored relationship with you in Jesus.

Let this time of worship be your time. Beyond our human participation, may we experience in our hearts all that is in your heart for us. Give us grace to respond to all that you reveal through the inspiration of your Holy Spirit. For Jesus' sake.

186

Lord God, prayers at the close of day have been offered by all generations of your people. We, who bow in worship and adoration, offer praise for the warmth of the day, and also thank you for the lengthening shadows which bring this evening hour.

The darkness which surrounds this place is lessened by the warm glow of light from our windows, and we are reminded that Jesus came — the light of the world. May we, his people, reflect the warmth of the beauty of Jesus in this community.

We offer our thanks to you, Lord, for your gift of light and love to the world. We are here to renew our own spirits; to feel the power of your forgiveness; and to seal again our promises to be your people.

We worship you with glad hearts, and we ask that you will accept our offerings of prayer and praise in this time together. In the name of Jesus Christ our Lord we pray.

187

O Lord, the majestic poetry of the psalmist gives us voice for praise when we say:

> Great is the Lord and greatly to be praised . . .
> for this God is our God for ever and ever.

The tender confessions of the psalmist have an echo in our own experience when we say:

> Have mercy upon me, O God, according unto your
>   loving kindness . . .
> Create in me a clean heart, O God, and renew a right
>   spirit within me.

We who worship here this evening express both these feelings — praise for your greatness, and petition for your forgiveness.

There are many who need our loving thoughts this evening . . .

> family members who are far away,
> fellow travellers who have lost their way,
> friends who have drifted away —
>   for each of them we pray;
> for those who are sick, we pray,
> for those all alone today,
> for the lost — help them to find a way
> to return to God,
>   we pray.

In this evening hour we will join in songs of praise. We will study your word for guidance and inspiration. We will be enriched by the melodies and harmonies of sacred music. Please God, help us to gain encouragement and hope through all these elements of worship.

Thank you for Jesus, our Saviour and intercessor, in whose name we offer our prayer.

188

Our Father, how good it is to call you 'Father', to know that you eagerly wait for us to gather around you, just as a loving father draws his little ones into the circle of his arms. We step closer, knowing that you are delighted we have come.

Accept our praise for all that you are — Creator, God, the Holy One — and yet, our Father. Though you are endlessly creating, preserving and governing all things, you are never too busy to listen to our voices, which to us seem weak and tedious, yet are sweet to your ears. With our lips and with our hearts, we say 'Thank you'.

Thank you for every evidence of your love; every nuance of your daily grace surrounding us; for the blessings of this life which you intend for our delight and growth; for providing all that we need. And beyond that, you have given us so often the desires of our hearts as we have learned to trust completely in you.

As we honour and worship you together with our brothers and sisters, help us to grow in unity and purpose. Help us to make glad your heart, your Father's heart that loves all children with a deep, strong love. Convict us of petty self-seeking, of all sin that separates us from you, and which diminishes us as your children.

In the name of your Son and our Saviour, Jesus Christ.

189

Father in heaven, we meet in your name to acknowledge your love and concern for all peoples. We remind ourselves of the depth of that love, which touches the human condition and seeks all who are missing your loving care. We rejoice with those who have experienced forgiveness and are saved from sin.

We are grateful for your plan of salvation — for sending Jesus Christ, your only Son, to become our Saviour — for giving us understanding of our sinful condition — and for allowing us the will to choose salvation, by seeking forgiveness through the sacrifice which was offered by Christ for our sins.

We pray that we may fulfil the divine purpose for our lives, and bring honour and glory to your cause and Kingdom in all things.

We praise your name, and give thanks for your blessings. Grant to us the joy and privilege of leading others to Christ, in whose name we pray.

190

Our Father, we have come into your house this evening because we recognise the encouragement and support which comes from joining with fellow Christians in a united act of worship.

We have come into your house this evening because we enjoy praising you; we are strengthened by praying together; we are enriched by each other's testimony to your grace; and through worship we learn new truths. All this helps us to grow in our experience and understanding of you.

We have come into your house this evening because so often before in this place we have known your presence in a real and wonderful way. We are come, therefore, with a sense of anticipation and expectancy, believing that you have something special for each of us.

Give us open minds, sensitive hearts, and the spirit of awareness, we pray.

191

Dear Father God, we are gathered in this place tonight to worship you, to praise you, to show our love for you. We are here to open your word and to learn more about you.

Help us to quieten our minds and calm our hearts. Be present with us as we concentrate on you. Let us be still before you.

O God, we praise you for the gift of your written word, which sustains and quickens our spirits. We thank you for your glorious grace, and for what it can do in our lives. We thank you for the gift of your Son, your only beloved Son — for Jesus, who personifies your grace, your undeserved favour. Show us again Jesus as he truly is. May we see him as the first disciples saw him. May he be as real to us as he was to them.

Bring us to the cross tonight, Lord. Let us see what it meant to Jesus, and what it now means for us. Help us to see the Christ as God and Lord, and to know that all the power in the universe is in him. Then we shall be ready for the Holy Spirit. Then we shall be ready to open to you, to each other, to the rest of the world. Then we shall be ready for there to be in our lives a process of unlimited change, through your undeserved favour. Then all the devious paths of our minds shall become straight. Then we shall be able to live in the light, as members one of another.

O God, let our lives be fulfilled individually and collectively within the fellowship of your Son Jesus. May we listen and hear the wonderful story of Jesus. Grant, Lord, that we shall not only listen and hear, but that we might believe and be changed.

O God, hear our earnest prayers, through Jesus Christ our Lord.

After the offering

192

Father, you are the giver of all gifts that we hold in trust. Accept, we pray, the marks of our stewardship:

> the thought of our minds;
> the labour of our hands;
> the love of our hearts;
> and these our gifts which are tokens of thought, labour
>   and love.

May our offering be used to enlarge your Kingdom, and so enrich those for whom we pray and for whom Christ died.

193

O God, you continually supply all our needs, according to the riches of your glory in Christ Jesus.

Make us, we pray, channels of your grace into the lives of others. We ask that we may never fail you nor our fellow men by allowing those channels to be blocked by our selfishness, greed or apathy.

Accept the offering we bring just now, and may it be a means by which we serve the world and disclose the love of Jesus.

194

Accept, O Lord, these gifts from our hands. With them receive also the worship and love of our hearts. Help us daily to live in the spirit of stewardship and of service.

'So shall no part of day or night from sacredness be free; but all our lives, in every part, be fellowship with thee.

In the name of Christ we tell the gratitude of our hearts for all of life's benefits, remembering always the needs of others.

195

We thank you, O Lord of life, for the life within us and for the life all around us.

We thank you for friends on earth and friends above; for all gentle thoughts and mild.

We thank you for work to do, for our homes and families, for health of mind and of body.

Here in the offering, are the symbols of our gratitude. Give us each an ever more grateful heart, a daily sense of stewardship, and always an openness to the needs of others.

196

Accept, O Lord, the gifts of our hands, and receive with them the love of our hearts; with the love of our hearts, receive also the dedication of our lives. All we possess comes from you, for we are but stewards of what we have and are.

As accountable stewards, and as your loving children, we bring our gifts and ourselves this day, in the name of Jesus Christ.

197

Dear heavenly Father, you are a generous God who has never withheld your hand from benefiting your children.

Thank you for allowing us to share and to grow by our giving.

Help us to appreciate the value of being able to give. Bless all who have given with a cheerful heart. We know that you cherish cheerful givers. You bless them more than many who may have seemingly received much.

Use our portion for your purposes, and we will continually praise your name.

198

Giver of all good things, we thank you:
    for health and strength;
    for the air that gives us the breath of life;
    and for the sun that warms us;
    for the good food that nourishes us;
    for happy homes and for friends to love;
    for all that makes it good to be alive.

Make us thankful, we pray, and eager to repay
    by cheerfulness and kindness and a readiness to help
        others.

Freely we have received; let us as freely give, in the name
of him who gave his life for us, Jesus Christ our Lord.

199

Divine Spendthrift on our behalf,
who has created with such abandonment
the wonders and marvels of our world,
and lavished such infinite love upon us,

Help us to use this opportunity
to respond with hearts of gratitude
and faithful stewardship.

Save us from the kind of thrift
or withholding that would impoverish.

May we show our love and loyalty
to you by the quality of our giving.

Closing prayers and benedictions

200

In the fellowship of the Holy Spirit we have gathered together;

By the broken body and shed blood of the the Lord Jesus Christ we have received new grace;

Through the love of the Father we have experienced mercy and forgiveness for our sins.

As we go into the world, may the living God live within our hearts, and be made known in our words and in our works; and may each new day bring us nearer to the joys unspeakable, in the blessedness of Heaven.

201

Dear Father, it has been so good to gather as a family with you. Soon we will depart and be scattered as seed from the sower's hand, scattered out there in the darkness.

May we each be as lights in that darkness, and should we feel a loneliness at our place of work, in our home or in our neighbourhood, help us to know the reality of your presence, and to remember our brothers and sisters who, just where *they* are, share in our labours and loneliness.

202

Lord, we are so precious to you. Even when we fail to think of you, there is not a moment in any day when any one of us is forgotten by you.

As we leave this place, we ask that in a real way you will make us aware of your company, your concern and your compassion. May we respond with lives that are lived to bring joy to the heart of our Father God. In the name of Jesus we pray.

203

Thank you, Lord, for the time we have spent in worship together. Each of us is unique; each of us came here with a private world of hopes and fears. Your love has drawn us together.

Your Spirit has given us new hopes, new thoughts, new insights. Help us to live in your love, and to share your goodness with others.

Some of us may leave with fears to face, with problems unsolved, with pain unremoved. May we also find that this time of worship has brought us new strength and hope and faith.

We ask it all in the name of Jesus who died for us and who lives with us.

204

Even after all these years, our Lord, we are still amazed that you entrust to the likes of us your magnificent mission for the Church.

We are grateful for the certainty of your call and for the joy of our service.

Help us, we pray, constantly and unswervingly to focus on those greater things for which you have formed your Church, and to which you have called us.

Now, as we depart, grant us courage and faith, inner peace and grace.

In the name of Jesus, your Son, our Saviour, we pray.

205

We wrap ourselves round in the creative energy of the Father, in the passionate love of the Son, and the enabling wisdom of the Spirit.

206

Father, may we let you detain us in all goodness of thought, word and deed.

Great Spirit of wisdom, may all of our lives be further education. Maintain in each of us a learning space, and keep us teachable.

In the name of the Son, Jesus Christ, we pray.

207

O faithful Lord, grant us we pray faithful hearts devoted to you and to the service of all people for your sake. Fill us with pure love for you, and keep us steadfast in this love. Give us faith that works by love, and preserve us faithful unto death. We pray this in the name of Jesus Christ our Lord.

Sunday-school and young people's meetings

208

Dear God, today we stand before you — the young people of your Kingdom. We are here to worship you, and to show you our love.

Every day, we strive for a good world, but become lost in material desires, and the wish to belong.

We search for respect in all the wrong things.

We want to be a better generation than the last, but times change and we face new challenges.

We long for a world of peace and unity, where differences of race, religion, sex or creed impose no barriers on our relationships with one another.

Give us your blessing today, and help us to achieve these things, through your love.

209

Father God

We are here just now for several different reasons. Some of us have come mainly to see our friends. Others of us want to discover more about you. There may be some of us didn't want to be here, but have been pressurised into coming to this meeting.

Just now, we ask that we shall feel your love and care for us in such a real way that we shall be glad you are our heavenly Father, and that we are your children.

Help us to get to know you better, and understand ourselves more, for when this happens life becomes more exciting and different.

We want this meeting to be happy, a meeting not only with our friends, but also with you. So please help us to put our best into it. For Jesus' sake.

210

O God, you are a great God. You answer when we call, and you never leave us.

You created us, and have given us great things. We thank you that you gave us Jesus, who died to save us from our sins.

We can never repay you, but we offer ourselves to you, and ask that you will accept us.

211

O God, you are a great God! When I need you, you are always there to comfort me. You pick me up when I fall. When I try to run away from you, you always know where I am. You know my every move. Before I knew myself, you knew me.

You created the world and everything in it. You made trees for the birds to build their nests in, and sing. You made grass for the cattle to eat. You created such a beautiful world. But man has destroyed so much of its beauty by sin.

You forgive sins. We praise you, O God.

Thank you for giving us Jesus. Thank you that he was sacrificed for our wrongdoings.

212

Good morning, God! It's great to be alive. We can meet together because you love us each one. Please look at how much energy we have, and help us use it to praise you, and to do things that will help our community. For Jesus' sake.

213

Dear God, you are worthy of greater love than we can give. We praise you for your eternal love in Jesus Christ. We ask you to be with us just now as we meet together.

We want our singing to express our praise to you.

We also ask that you will open our minds to understand what the Bible lesson means.

Jesus welcomed children in Palestine as you now welcome us, and we thank you that we are alive, and can learn about you.

Help us to trust you. And help us to remember to pray. In Jesus' name.

214

Dear God, we are known by names. We have the nicknames that our friends call us; pet names that our families call us; names of those who we are in our games.

Help us to believe that you know who we really are, and that who we really are is very important to you.

Help us also to recognise you in all the names we use for you in our prayers.

Women's meetings

215

Dear Lord, we have come into this place to meet together as friends; friends from different kinds of homes, and different kinds of families, with different kinds of hopes and joys and doubts and problems. And yet we know, Lord, that today we shall find so much that we have in common — things we have in common because we are women — wives and mothers and daughters and sisters.

Help us, we pray, to rejoice and be grateful for our differences, which make us what we are; and help us also to be glad and to find strength in the bonds which unite us.

May our meeting today lift us nearer to yourself, as we worship. May we learn some new thing to take away with us into our daily lives, something that will enrich us and benefit our homes. May the fellowship which we share remind us each that in times of loneliness or perplexity there are good friends to whom we can turn for advice, or for a comforting arm on which to lean. May we find fun and laughter and let our minds turn away for a while from the demands which we have left, and to which we shall return.

As we look around our company, Lord, we see that there are empty seats, seats which are usually occupied by members of our fellowship. Some are ill, or tending others that are ill; some have duties that cannot be left; some, perhaps, have a problem that they feel unwilling to bring with them to the meeting. For all of these, our sisters in Christ, we pray, and ask that should they need our support in any way, they will not find us wanting.

This is our special time together, Lord, and we commend it to you, asking that we shall use it wisely and well. When we leave, may we feel better in body, mind and spirit than when we arrived. For Jesus' sake.

216

Lord, women were among those who saw you alive on that first Easter Day. You took time to speak to the woman of Samaria at the well. On the day of Pentecost your Holy

Spirit was poured out on both men and women. You made it so clear in your day that you wished to use us all for your glory.

Lord Jesus, we are here today in your house, and we want to know your presence and hear you speaking to us. We come to you with confidence because we know that you care. We want to thank you for all that you do for us. But today some of us are really burdened. Some of us are sad because of family problems. Some of us carry heavy anxiety. There are so many needs in our midst. We ask you to understand and help us.

Please, by your Holy Spirit, illuminate your word. Teach us. Let us feel that we are face to face with you.

Help us, Lord, to encourage each other, and offer a helping hand when we see a need. Make us alert to see the face of loneliness.

Bless our families. And bless us here, as an extended family. In Jesus' name we ask our prayers.

217

O God, our gracious Saviour, to whom we belong and whom we serve, we bow in your presence in love and adoration.

We are mindful that we follow in the steps of those women who long ago followed you through the dust of Galilee, stood by the cross, and were first at the tomb on the resurrection morning. We are proud to belong to the vast company who from that time to the present day have kept the Christian faith alive.

Help us to have faith like the Syro-Phoenician woman; devotion like Mary who anointed your feet with ointment; a practical mind like Martha, who was blessed in household ways.

In our prayerful and practical concerns for worthy causes in the wider world, let us also be mindful of the needy people in our own locality: lonely women and children in need of friendship; minority groups who may find difficulty with our culture and our language; little ones and young people from broken families; those living alone after divorce and separation; and so many others who are victims of society or of their own weaknesses.

May we be ready to open our homes in Christian hospitality as part of our commitment to you.

We rejoice that in your Kingdom there is no racial discrimination; no cultural discrimination; no social discrimination; no sex discrimination. But all are one and precious in your sight.

May we not only follow you, but love you with a constant mind, and lose ourselves to save mankind.

We pray in the lovely name of Jesus.

218

Dear Father in Heaven, we come before you with hearts full of anticipation. We look forward to a joyful time of worship and fellowship in your presence. We prayed, and our leaders spent many hours in preparation for this time together. Thank you, Lord, for the dedicated creativity which has made our gathering possible. Thank you for all who will participate. Relieve them of any nervousness, and assure them of your calming presence.

Prepare our hearts and minds to accept every possible blessing from this day. May our eyes and ears be opened to your leadership.

In Jesus' name we pray.

219

Dear heavenly Father, our hearts rejoice over the evidence of your Holy Spirit among us. Thank you for speaking to women who need so much to hear your voice.

Our needs are great and varied. We live in a time of confusion about our roles and responsibilities. Sometimes the demands of home and family compete with those at work and church. There never seems enough time or energy to do all that is expected of us.

Thank you, Lord, for this opportunity to come apart from hectic activity into your quiet presence. Assure us of your desire that we should live calm and ordered lives. Give us the wisdom and courage to change our pace, according to your will.

To those women who seek pardon from sin, grant grace to accept your forgiveness. To those who are burdened for husbands, children or friends, bring peace of mind and heart. Instruct them daily in ways of sensitive witnessing. Help us all to be good examples of your love to those who look to us in time of need. May we always be aware of your willingness to supply us from your unlimited resources, that we may share your blessings with others.

As we leave this place of worship, go with us, we pray. Teach us to live the kind of life you had in mind for us when you created us. Help us to be content, and to rejoice in the unique opportunities we have as Christian women.

We ask these favours in Jesus' name.

220

O God, we come into your presence, and thank you for the pleasure we have in being together in this way.

We thank you for the friendship and understanding we share here. We feel comfortable and accepted, and somehow feel better able to face the demands of daily living.

Today, we are aware of those who depend on us — on our provision and our care; on our help and our guidance — and we are aware also of those who are influenced by our words, our actions, and our attitudes.

At times, we feel their dependence like a weight upon our shoulders. Some days, it seems almost too heavy. And then, O God, we remember that you have promised your strength to those who lean on you.

Help us today, we pray, to discover afresh your limitless resources, which are always available to us. Help us to depend upon you totally, and to experience again your ability to meet all our needs.

And, as we depend upon you, may those who depend on us discover our secret strength for themselves.

We pray for this in the name of Jesus.

221

Our Father, as we meet today we thank you for the gift of communication, which enables us to relate to each other in so many different ways.

We thank you for the gift of speech, the ability to share conversation with our friends. We can talk together about the things that concern and interest us. We can exchange opinions and ideas. We can enjoy laughter.

We thank you too because we can communicate through silence, when words are futile and inadequate. At such times we can share a loving smile, a warm handshake, and a comforting arm.

During this time together, we recognise the importance of our ministry to each other, through giving and receiving in a spirit of companionship, friendship and worship.

More than all else, we thank you because we can commune with you, and you are central to all that we shall do today.

222

O God, Lord of all in Heaven and on earth, we praise you for our unique place in your creation. We praise you for the specific roles and abilities given to women — for the distinctive female nature and attitude, inclination and insight. We acknowledge these gifts from you, and rejoice in them.

And so, we earnestly seek wisdom, inspiration and guidance from you, that not one of these precious gifts might be betrayed, under-used, distorted.

Grant, Lord, that each of us, alert to our true vocation, will nobly and in godly demeanour fulfil all the holy purposes for which you have made us.

Fill our hearts with tender love of your people, and our minds with noble and lofty thoughts. Shape our wills to heavenly endeavours in earthly places, and our purposes to your purpose.

Thus shall we women make a unique place in your creation — a holy place.

Senior citizens' meetings

223

Dear heavenly Father, we thank you for this social gathering, which we enjoy so much, and we thank you that we have the means and the ability to attend. We thank you for all the blessings and mercies which have been ours on life's journey. As we look back along the way, we can see, perhaps as we failed to see at the time, that you were always there to help us and to meet our needs.

Today, Lord, some of us are struggling a little. Some of us know pains and aches that we never dreamed could be possible. For others, no two days are the same; after a good day, we dread waking up in case the pain or the sickness are back again. Please, Lord, don't think that we are always complaining and ungrateful, but our troubles are so very real to us. Some of us live alone, and there is no one but you with whom we can share our difficulties. And you did say: 'Come unto me, all you who are troubled and carry heavy burdens.' Dear Lord, please come and bless us as we meet together, to reassure us of your care and understanding.

We give you our thanks for the many ways in which you do bless our ways: we have family and friends and food and homes; there are things to see and taste and touch and hear and smell. Help us to concentrate our minds upon the blessings we have, rather than upon our difficulties, no matter how bad they seem to be.

Today, may we make our business that of bringing joy to our friends here, in the knowledge that real happiness is most possessed by those who give it to others. In the name of Jesus we pray.

224

Lord, we praise you for the experience of the present days in which we live. We thank you for the blessing of retirement, for the release from pressure which we enjoy, for the opportunity to take delight in the created world, for a larger measure of time to think and to read and to pray.

171

We thank you that your will and way for us know no end. We bless you for the many opportunities of service still open to us. We praise you for new vision and new thoughts given to us so bountifully. Especially we thank you for the privilege of intercession for others.

We come to you now in petition for your world. We see it so obsessed by fear, so troubled by threats of doom. We see it so torn by strife and hatred, so full of suffering and despair. Help us by your grace to lift up a voice of hope and promise, to believe and trust in your dominion, assured that the world, our dear ones, and we ourselves are in your strong and loving hands.

Lord, we pray for the Church into which you have called us. We thank you for its message of salvation for all mankind, for its teaching about holy living, for its high ideals of selfless service. We thank you for the place you have assigned to us within it. We pray for our leaders, that all strength and grace may be given to them. We pray for Christians everywhere, that the call to renewal may reach all hearts. Pour out your blessing upon the Church, that your Kingdom may come within it and through it, and that it may be used for the redemption of the world.

Lord, renew our hearts, our faith, and our purpose this day.

225

Lord, we bless you that we are able to look toward the future with hope and joy. We believe that in your eternal providence the best is yet to be. We can expect greater manifestations of your love, a deeper knowledge of the unsearchable riches of Christ, and unfolding of mysteries which now perplex us, a scattering of darkness, and answering of questionings and fears.

We thank you that though our outward man may perish, yet the inward is renewed day by day. Though our physical powers fail, yet our inner life is strengthened. Spiritual ageing can mean clearer sight and insight, greater maturity, new growth. We praise you that we know these things by experience.

Preserve in us a sense of humour, and maintain us in thankfulness. Help us, when we must, to accept the weakening of bodily strength and to believe that there is more life and more love ahead, new horizons opening for us, new frontiers to cross. May Heaven be in us before we are in Heaven.

Lord, we believe for the future of the Church and its influence in the world. Make us worthy of the name we bear, the responsibilities which are ours and the call you make to us.

Help us to take new courage from the assurance that in all things we are more than conquerors through him that loved us.

226

Dear heavenly Father, thank you for bringing us today to this place of love and friendship. We pray that as we share another day together, it will be a special time, when we shall be made aware of your great love for us all. We thank you that through Jesus Christ, you have made it possible for us to know you. We pray that today you will give us all a new understanding of how we can love you.

May this meeting bring us much pleasure and delight. Help us to focus on the joys of fellowship and belonging. Help us to remember that you are the one who brings us true joy and happiness. Here is an opportunity for us to consider your greatness and your goodness.

For the people here who are facing disappointments, physical weakness, family problems, personal anxieties and other difficulties, we pray for a special touch of your love. May they realise that you know all about them, understand their needs, and are very near to help and support them. May they know that Jesus comes to all who reach out a hand in faith for him to touch and to heal.

Thank you for everyone who works to make these meetings a special time for us all. For those who prepare the hall, for those who work in the kitchen, for those who drive vehicles to bring people here — may they all be blessed for their service given in your name.

We pray that our community will feel the love of this place, as we go out from here to share the good news of what you have done for us, and what you are to us. We pray in Jesus' name.

Business meetings

227

Lord, we pray for your presence
and guidance at our business meeting.

We confess that often we have had
misgivings about such meetings —
their seeming ineffectiveness,
the claim of other priorities
on our energies and time.

Often, our words filled the air,
minutes were tidily added to the files,
and we returned to 'business as usual'.

But help us just now with
a perception for our task,
a sensitivity to needs,
courage to think independently
and to speak honestly.

Enable us to translate
our words into action,
our rhetoric into deeds,
our planning into fulfilment,
our insights into involvement,
our convictions into commitments.

We pray in the name of Jesus,
Lord of all our life and activity.

At the dedication of an infant

228

Almighty God, Father of us all, we bring before you in prayer this little child .... (He/She) has been presented to this congregation today with the intention that (he/she) shall be raised in the knowledge of the Lord Jesus Christ, and according to the principles of the Christian faith.

We pray that you will honour the dedication of this child by receiving (him/her) into the fellowship of your Church on earth. Upon the parent(s) we ask that you will place your hand of blessing, giving grace to keep the promises which have been made today in the presence of your people.

Our fondest hope for this little one is that (he/she) shall quickly take hold of saving grace, and so make personal (his/her) allegiance to Jesus Christ. As this child of yours and of ours advances in years, so may (he/she) grow in the understanding of the Lord Jesus Christ. Our Father God, we know that (he/she) is entering an uncertain and confusing world, a world in which Jesus is not readily given a place. May (he/she) early learn the power of prayer, and the abiding presence of your Holy Spirit.

Give (him/her), we pray, clear vision, constant faith, unfaltering hope and abounding love.

In his name we pray who called little ones to himself to be blessed, the name of Jesus Christ our Lord.

229

Dear Father God, the giver of every good and perfect gift, we thank you especially today for the joy and beauty you have brought into the world with this little child.

As (he/she) learns to love and understand the mysteries of the created world, may (he/she) also come to a saving knowledge of its Creator, and so share in the glories of a world unseen.

Through Jesus Christ our Lord.

230

Loving heavenly Father, we thank you that it is part of your design for your world that we should live together in families, and we are grateful for this opportunity to bring a new member of the family into your house.

Take (him/her) into your keeping, and give divine wisdom and understanding to all who have an influence in (his/her) life.

In Jesus' name.

231

Dearest heavenly Father, giver of all good gifts, we praise your name for the gift of this precious child.

We know and acknowledge that all children are born for you. We own no one and no one owns us — but in your kindness you allow us to tend your precious ones for a season.

Bless the parents who act as your stewards; bless the family members who will help to model and encourage; bless the friends who share in the wonder of this dedication.

Lord, grant your wisdom to all who endeavour to show Christ's love to this child. Grant growth, health and spiritual understanding to your young servant.

In Jesus' name we pray.

232

Our loving Father, we come to you in the name of Jesus, the friend of little children. You are the giver of every good and perfect gift, and our lives have been enriched by your generosity to us. We acknowledge with gratitude the gift of children. The family is your idea, Father, and it is with a deep sense of thankfulness that we present this little child to you.

Our hearts are moved when we remember Jesus' love for children, how he took them in his arms and blessed them. Because of that, this act of dedication on the part of the parents has great significance. It is an acknowledgment of their gratitude and worship. As this child has been brought to your house today, we pray that you will accept the parents' offering of love.

It is our prayer that they may be given wisdom, patience, and a deeper understanding of you as they bring up this child. We thank you for their devotion, and for their desire to teach and train little .... in the ways of God. We would also pray that this child will develop in body and mind, and bring a great deal of joy to all the family. Because of the example of Christian living in the home, it should not be difficult for this little one to find Jesus as Saviour and friend early in life.

Set your seal upon this dedication, as we make our request in the name of Jesus.

233

Father, this day we offer a prayer as we dedicate this little new life .... In (him/her) we see the hand of the master Creator, and we are reminded once again of your faith in the human race. Here, O Lord, is surely the beauty and culmination of love, expressed in the form of a tiny baby.

In some ways, Lord, we would want to keep the child just like this, small and safe and protected from the greed and evil of this world, but we know that is not possible. We know that (he/she) must grow to childhood and adolescence in an environment contaminated by sin. We would pray then that you will watch over (his/her) life and living.

Father, protect this child from the false values and materialism that are so influential and powerful in our world today, and grant that (he/she) may seek those qualities in life which have eternal value.

Guide and direct the parents as they counsel and discipline. Grant them great grace, wisdom and limitless love, that they may convey to .... the example that (he/she) will need to mould and establish (his/her) own values and personality.

In Jesus' name we offer our prayers.

234

Lord Jesus, who when upon earth
took the children into your arms,
embraced them, and smiled upon them,
and spoke tender words of blessing to them,

So take .... into your arms of love;
give the warmth of your smile
and your own gracious word of blessing.

Grant the hallowed presence
of the Holy Spirit
to protect this child from evil,
and guide (him/her) in your pathway,
where alone are true happiness and peace.

Bless the parents,
that they may seek first your Kingdom
and your righteousness,
and build a home where your
love and peace shall reign.

235

Eternal Father, we thank you for your great love, and for the concern you show for your people, as they seek to be fulfilled through parenthood.

You have blessed our dear friends with a beautiful baby. We thank you that this child has the capacity to smile and to cry, to respond to sound, and to enjoy the wonderful world you have provided.

Your blessing is sought for this baby, and we believe your protection and provision will be given.

Empower the parents with heavenly wisdom, that they might train their child to love you, and to seek your ways daily. Through Jesus Christ, our Lord.

At the public initiation of a new adult Christian

236

Almighty God, you are the Father of all mankind, and by the dying love of your Son you have made possible the salvation of the world.

As a company of your people we have this day witnessed the declaration of one who acknowledges a saving faith in

Jesus Christ, and who professes that same Jesus Christ to be Lord and Saviour in *(his/her) life.

In our presence, our (brother/sister) in Christ has entered into solemn undertakings. We rejoice with (him/her) in all (his/her) hopes, aspirations and commitments. May divine strength be (his/hers) each day, to meet each day's needs. Help us, O God, to keep faith with ...., bearing (him/her) up in our prayers and giving strength with our words of encouragement. (He/She) has recognised that only by your grace can (he/she) fulfil the vows that have been made this day; yet at the same time we know that the lives of God's people here below can hinder or help .... in (his/her) walk with Christ. Therefore, we pray, keep us true to our own commitment as we make our inward renewal of faith.

As we receive .... into our worshipping family, we pray that you will receive (him/her) into the company of your saints below. May (his/her) work and witness and all (his/her) living be for the salvation of the world and the glory of the gospel, through Jesus Christ our Saviour.

* masculine, feminine or plural usages, as appropriate

237

O God, our Father, we rejoice that you gave your Son, Jesus Christ, for the salvation of the world. We thank you for *those gathered here this day, who in your presence and in the presence of Christian friends, have pledged themselves to the service of the Church of Christ on earth.

182

We pray that they will constantly claim your grace to fulfil the promises which they have made, knowing that their continuance in a state of salvation depends upon their continued obedient faith in you.

Will you daily strengthen their resolve to live for you, and in so doing may they find fulfilment and joy.

We remember and praise you for those who, by precept and by practice, have influenced the commitments made this day.

We ask that this ceremony, an outward token in which we have all shared, will encourage us to pray for and to support one another in and through the power of your Holy Spirit. May we each one strive to be true soldiers of Jesus Christ.

Our prayers we offer in the name of God the Father, the Son, and the Holy Spirit.

* singular usage, if appropriate

238

Just where he needs me,
My Lord has placed me,
Just where he needs me, there would I be!
And since he found me,
By love he's bound me
To serve him joyfully.

This is a sacred moment, O God. We feel the power of your presence. We sense the thrill of emotion as

.... (*or* these our friends, etc) publicly identifies with our Lord Jesus Christ as a true soldier of his.

Life-changing promises have been made and signed before many witnesses — but signing is not sacrifice! Keep .... true to those promises, we pray, even in the face of hardship.

Thank you, Lord, for the supreme privilege of Christian service. May this new soldier of Jesus Christ find total joy and complete satisfaction in selfless service.

239

O Lord, the call of Christ echoes through the ages, and in every generation there have been those individuals who have heard and answered that call.

We stand in your presence as witnesses to the recurring miracle of lives transformed by the power of your love.

And now — this new soldier of Jesus Christ has sealed the promise to serve you faithfully, joyfully!

By the power of the Holy Spirit, may ....
    have a heart to love unconditionally,
    a voice to speak of that love eloquently,
    a life to live in that love eternally.

We pray in the strong name of Jesus.

At a marriage service

240

O God, our Father, whose greatest gift is love, bless .... and .... who today within your presence will give themselves to each other in marriage.

We thank you that they have found such love, faith and trust that they wish to commit themselves to one another for all the days of their lives.

We pray that nothing will come between them that will prevent them from being forever faithful and forever true.

Grant that each may be to the other a strength in need, a counsellor in perplexity, a comfort in sorrow and a companion in joy.

May they both ever love you, and as they seek to live in harmony and peace may they at all times seek first your Kingdom.

241

God of love, from whom comes every good and perfect gift, bless .... and .... whom you have this day joined together in marriage.

As they kneel before you in gratitude, trust and hope, sanctify their union by your Holy Spirit. Deepen their love and strengthen their faith.

May their home be radiant with joy and peace, and may your word, and your perfect will, determine the pattern of all their days.

By your grace, may they live together in a bond of rich companionship and faithfulness, through the name and the grace of Jesus Christ our Lord.

242

Dearest Lord Jesus, you who sanctified the rite of marriage as it was ordained by God your Father, we praise your name.

We thank you for this precious union of two lives that have now joined as one.

We praise you for the pledges made, the vows exchanged, and the love professed.

We seek your favour for these who have left father and mother to cling and to cleave to each other. Bless their purposes and intents as they are surrendered to be embroidered into your perfect will.

Further this family, as it pleases you to do. Extend their influence, and remember them as they remember you.

Help them in time of trial. Keep and reconcile them when they are tempted to stray. Guide them that they might model the highest concepts of marriage to others, and by so doing may they bless your name and extend your Kingdom.

In your holy name we pray.

243

O God our Father, giver of grace and wisdom, set your seal upon this solemn act.

Give your blessing to .... and .... as they stand at the threshold of a new and holy relationship.

Help them to keep the sacred promises they have made this day.

Grant that they may ever love you and live in peace and harmony; and that in all circumstances they may seek first your Kingdom.

This we ask through Jesus Christ our Lord.

244

Our Father, we thank you for your gift of love, in all its many and varied forms, and for the way in which love enhances each of our lives every day.

On this special day, we thank you for the gift of love which you have placed in the hearts of .... and ...., and which has brought them to this time when they desire to commit themselves to each other, and to you.

More than all else, we would pray for them in these precious moments a real sense of your nearness, the assurance of your grace and strength, your wisdom and your leading as they enter this lifelong partnership.

We know that
Your presence will add to their joys;
Your presence will ease their disappointments;
Your presence will confirm their decisions;
Your presence will calm their confusions;
Your presence will deepen their understanding of, and love
        for, each other;
Your presence will enrich their togetherness;
Your presence will make their union complete.

May they and we know your presence in our lives today.
We pray in Jesus' name.

245

Our Father, we pray for ....and ....
who have come to ask you to seal and bless their marriage
covenant.

It is in your loving plan for us that men and women should
enter into such a covenant, to pledge loyalty and devotion
for a lifetime together.

It is in your design that Christian homes should be
established — homes based on love and appreciation for
each other, whilst reaching out in hospitality, and making
room for others.

As this ceremony is the beginning of a new life together,
we ask that you will be with .... and
.... as they make the small and large
compromises that will be required to weld together two
separate personalities into a workable unity. Give them
patience and forbearance, we ask.

We who love them pray for them. May mutual caring and consideration keep their marriage young. May their loyalty and devotion to each other never fail, and may they find their spiritual lives constantly renewed through their individual and united service for you.

Grant them the strength of fidelity, the leavening of humour, and the gentleness of mutual consideration.

Above all, grant them the continuing certainty of knowing the presence of your Holy Spirit. We pray these things in the name of Jesus, our Lord.

246

O God, our loving Father, we come with great joy in our hearts, and thank you for the love and mercy you have shown to us all.

We thank you because you have led .... and .... to this special moment in their lives. We thank you because they have experienced your grace, and believe it is your will that they take this step, and accept the gift of marriage which you give them today.

We thank you for this wonderful gift, for the privilege it gives of being committed at the greatest level of human experience to one whom we love the most; and for the opportunity it presents of developing a loving relationship of quality and depth that has the potential to grow with time. We thank you, our Father, because you provide all the rich resources of your grace, so that this possibility can become a reality. We thank you for the new beginning which marriage represents; for all the joy, love, companionship and support it promises. We are aware, dear Father, that all growth means times of pain as well as joy. We would not ask that you spare our friends from any experience or test that has the capacity to help them grow, but rather would pray that you will enable them to **meet** every test.

May .... and .... experience your grace in their joy today, and in their future of adjustments and challenges. May they always be as keenly aware as they are now, standing in your presence, that this marriage is your loving purpose for them.

In the name of Jesus, our Saviour and Lord, we make our prayer.

247

Christ, the source and inspirer of our joys,
as centuries ago you came and
blessed the wedding feast at Cana,
so today come, we pray,
and be the honoured guest
at this happy and sacred occasion.

Grant the blessing of your presence
to our friends, who stand on the threshold
of a new life together.

Bless this husband ....
as provider for his family.
Sustain him in life's pressures.
May his love be ....'s joy,
his strength be her protection,
and his character be her pride.

Bless this wife ....
Give her a tender and loving heart,
a spirit of understanding,
an inner beauty of soul that never fades,
and a faith that never fails.

Help them not to expect the perfection
of each other that belongs only to you.
May they minimise each other's weaknesses,
and magnify each other's strengths.

Help them to deal tenderly
with each other's dreams.
Seeking first your Kingdom
and your righteousness,
may they live together in love and peace
in this world;
and in the world to come
obtain everlasting life,
though Jesus Christ, our Lord.

At a retirement of a married couple

248

Eternal God, the Alpha and Omega, Lord of our
beginnings and Lord of our endings, we thank you that
years ago you called out from the crowd a gifted young
man and young woman, our friends whom we honour this
day — .... and .... to be
your servants.

We thank you for keeping them faithful to their covenant, for their ministry of heart and hand, of leadership and love; for the lives they have touched as instruments of your love and peace.

Now, as they are released from the daily demands of official duties, as they come not to the end, but to a bend in their road of service, we pray that you will lead them into paths of creative retirement, crowned with grace and strength, the joys of family and friends, and with continued fulfilment in doing your will and work.

We pray in the name of the one who is the Alpha and Omega, the Lord of our beginnings and the Lord of our endings.

At a funeral service

249

O God, our Father, at such a time as this, we stand face to face with the things of eternity. At such a time as this, we become so aware of mankind's temporal nature. At such a time as this, we must ponder the reality of death, the awesomeness of your judgement, but also the glory of Christ's redemptive work.

The friend who is no longer with us has passed from what we call life into what we call death. We believe, although we have never seen, that this death may become a life greater than our imagining, a life that is *in* Christ and *with* Christ.

You, O God, know the truth about us all. Your justice and your mercy are strong, and we have committed the mortal remains of our friend to the elements, knowing that his soul's eternal destiny will be ordered according to your infinite wisdom.

As you are a God of justice and mercy and wisdom, so you are a God of compassion and grace. We therefore commend to your loving care those who today mourn the passing of one dear to them, those for whom there will be an empty place in the home and in the heart. Fill the emptiness, we pray, O God, with the fullness of your Holy Spirit, and may the resurrection grace of Jesus be their portion.

Grant to us each one a knowledge that to dwell in Christ is to have eternal life, and make this to be our heart's chief desire. In his name we pray.

250

Eternal God, our Creator and heavenly Father, we thank you for the life of our friend ...., whom you have called to be with you in the radiance of your presence. Whilst sorrow fills our hearts because (he/she) is no longer with us, we rejoice in (his/her) love for you, and for the enrichment we have received from this. Truly this love was graciously and effectively expressed in ministering to the needs of your people.

We come in confidence that our friend has heard your commendation, 'Well done, good and faithful servant', and is now serving you in Heaven. We believe that (he/she) now stands with the multitude around your throne, worshipping you in the glory of your presence.

As our dear friend was faithful to the Christ whose name (he/she) bore, may we also keep faith to the end of life's journey. We pray in the name of Jesus, who is resurrection and life.

251

O Father-God, in accordance with the assurance of your word, at this solemn and sacred time, we do not grieve as those who are without hope. We have confidence that through the resurrection of our Lord Jesus Christ death has lost its sting, and the grave has lost its victory.

In this certain awareness, we commit to your eternal care our (brother/sister) .... who has been taken from our presence, and who is now with you in Heaven. Thank you for the privilege which was ours of knowing a dear friend, and for every enrichment and joy which that friendship brought into our lives.

Grant us the peace which comes from your comfort in the midst of our sorrow. This we ask in the name of Jesus, who went to prepare a place for us.

252

Lord Jesus, we thank you for the gracious assurance you have given: 'Blessed are they that mourn, for they shall be comforted'. We are confident that you will support with your presence and understanding those who today feel such intense grief and loss.

You are sensitive to the tears which flow, since you also stood weeping over the death of a friend. May your comfort sustain those for whom we pray, not only now but in the days of loneliness which will surely lie ahead.

This we ask as we remember your promise, 'Peace I leave with you; my peace I give unto you. . . . Let not your heart be troubled, neither let it be afraid.'

253

O God, we would praise you for one whose life has been lived worthily. We give thanks for the fight well fought, the course finished, the faith kept, and the crown of righteousness received.

We praise you, and yet, mingled with our praise is human sorrow. This you understand, for we have not a high priest who cannot be touched with the feelings of our infirmities, but one who wept at the grave of a friend beloved. The vale of tears is no strange land to you, for in Christ and for our sakes you have travelled through it.

Now we pray that you will comfort those who mourn. May Heaven seem a nearer and dearer place because of a loved one gone ahead, and may the prospect of reunion in your presence be an added incentive for faithful service.

Then when the shadows lengthen and this life is near its end, may the life to come beckon as a new adventure with you, through Jesus Christ our Lord.

254

Our Father, we are meeting together to give thanks for the life of ....
We thank you for all that (he/she) meant to us.
We thank you for all our memories, some sad, but so many happy.
We thank you for (his/her) love and friendship, for every good deed done and for every kind word spoken.
We pray, Father, that the good (he/she) was able to do in this world might remain, and continue to bear fruit for you.

Help us now to release .... to you, (his/her) maker and judge, confident in the knowledge of your mercy and thankful for (his/her) life among us.

Thank you that you gave .... to us, and that you have now seen fit to take (him/her) from us. May we allow (him/her) to rest peacefully within our hearts, and may we treasure all our remembrances.

Our Father, we pray for those who mourn, especially ....
Comfort them and us in our grief, sustain us in our sorrow, and strengthen us in our weakness, we pray.
Remind us of Jesus, your Son, our Saviour, who also wept and suffered and died — and yet rose triumphant over death.
May we too triumph through him and with him, we pray.

Father, we commend each other to you at this sad time.
May the light of your love in Christ shine in our hearts through the darkness of our sorrow.
May we be a comfort and a strength to one another.

May each trouble of life draw us closer to you, God of all compassion and mercy.

We pray in Jesus' name.

255

Eternal God and everlasting Father, we come to you in the name of Jesus, your Son and our Saviour. The mystery of life and death is again before us — the reminder of our humanity and mortality.

Within our limitations, we come to you, our Creator, preserver, infinite and sovereign Lord.

You see your children weep. Through Jesus, you know so well our loneliness, hurt and profound sense of loss. You suffer with us.

It is with thankfulness that we remember the life of the one who has passed into eternity. Thank you for (his/her) contribution to our lives, for every expression of love and friendship. Human relationships are a gift from you — so precious, bringing quality and richness to our lives. We will miss the warmth of human communion, the smile, the embrace, the handshake, that unique personality.

The sting of death is very painful. We need your healing balm, the calm of your peace, your comfort in our pain and grief. Help us, dear Lord, in our suffering.

We grieve, but not as those without hope. Your word reassures us through Jesus, who said, 'I am the resurrection and the life. He who believes in me will live, even though he dies . . .'. Thank you, Lord, for that promise. Not even death can separate us from you.

The passing of our friend .... reminds us of our own soul's needs. Our human frame is so fragile, our hold on life so slender. We too must one day leave this world. We have no lasting citizenship here. We must look for the city which is to come. In the new dimension of Heaven, we shall find completeness. The flawed will be transformed to perfection, mortality be exchanged for immortality.

Dear Lord, through your grace, prepare us to meet you. Help us to endure the tears of the night, and to be courageous in the darkness, believing that joy will be ours in the morning.

We pray these prayers in the name of Jesus Christ, whom to know is life eternal.

256

Almighty God, there are many feelings that well up within our hearts today.

We feel the sense of unfairness that one in the prime of life should succumb to disease and be taken from us. We feel anger at this seeming injustice. We feel loneliness and loss. To whom can we go with our feelings? Human courage and fortitude have been displayed to the highest extent — but only you are Alpha and Omega: the beginning and the end.

So we bow before you, an understanding and comforting God. You know suffering in Jesus Christ, who died on the cross for our sakes. We humbly acknowledge that your wisdom is greater than ours, because you can see the end from the beginning. We can thank you that Jesus defeated death, so that we might share in his victory, and in the life to come. Your divine purposes will then be seen. All wrongs will be put to right, and suffering will be no more.

Until that day, we pray that your Holy Spirit will bring comfort to those who mourn, especially to .... and to all the family. We thank you for the precious memories they have of their loved one, from those good years before (his/her) illness. May those memories bring joy and not pain to their hearts.

We offer thanks for doctors and nursing staff, who with great skill and care did all that could possibly be done for .... We pray for those involved in medical service; may they receive all the encouragement they need to continue their labours. May your Holy Spirit lead into all truth those who work on the frontiers of the healing sciences.

We ask these our prayers in the name of Jesus Christ, the great physician.

At a memorial (or thanksgiving) service

257

O God, as we set aside this time to remember our dear friend ...., we realise that however many words we use, and whatever we find ourselves saying about (his/her) life, we shall not be able to recall adequately all that (he/she) has meant to us.

We thank you that you know all things, and that you are aware of the appreciation and thanksgiving that are in our hearts. We bring our remembrances to you, and ask that you will receive and bless them.

We pray especially for those who have been bereaved of a loved one. Their sense of loss reveals just how greatly .... was valued within the family. We ask you to comfort them as they mourn, and to reassure them of your great and eternal love.

As we give thanks for a life lived among us, we praise you for Jesus who, by his death and resurrection, has provided eternal life for all who will receive it. In his name we offer our thanksgiving and prayers.

258

Eternal Father, you have promised eternal life to all who believe in you. We meet to honour the life and memory of .... for whom we give thanks this day. In faith we have committed (him/her) to your keeping until that day when we shall rejoice together in your presence.

For those who mourn, we pray that they may experience the reassurance of your love, and the strength from friends who share in their grief. Through Jesus Christ, our Lord.

259

Eternal God, you conquered death through Jesus. Yet, our sense of triumph is tempered by our feelings of human loss. Our words sound empty, and we do not know how best to pray. Yet you see us and love us through the days of our grief. Strong Lord, you support us in our time of need, and for this we give you thanks.

260

O Lord, our God, we rejoice for the witness of ....'s life, for the influence of the good which was spread, and for (his/her) life of victory. We think of the years of faithful and cheerful service, the self-forgetfulness, and unflinching faith through good times and bad. We remember the example shown by this true servant of God, and lover of (his/her) fellow men. (He/She) is so sadly missed by family and by all of us, and we bring the family to you in our prayers.

May the lives of such men and women of faith continue to inspire your people in all walks of life. Help us each to take courage from our departed friend's example, and to stand and be counted. Lord, show your power in our individual lives, that we too may lead others to you. In the name of Jesus we pray.

Advent

261

Our heavenly Father, hearts everywhere are being strangely warmed again as this holy season is with us. May it be a time when barriers will be removed, and when your loving presence will be welcomed into lives that have never known you.

Help us not to become too busy with preparations that we forget to pray.

Incline the hearts of those estranged from home and family to make contact once again.

Let forgiveness flow to bridge the gulf of broken relationships.

Cause the eyes of your Church on earth to look and see in the darkened skies the continued promise of your coming.

Confirm within us the certainty of your return, so that we may be watching and waiting, without fear of what the future holds.

Help us to broadcast to a needy world that the Prince of Peace is still the guardian of his creation, and that one day the babe of Bethlehem will be acclaimed King of all kings.

262

O God our Father, we are glad for every anticipation of the Christmas season, for its light and laughter, its music and busyness, and for the prospect of reunion with family and friends.

We remember, however, that no adequate preparation had been made for the birth of Christ, and we meet here — with prayer and in penitence — to make special preparation, so that the real meaning of Christmas does not pass us by.

O God, our Father, we recall that the child born in Bethlehem grew to be the man who said that the birds of the air had their nests, that foxes had their lairs, but that, he had nowhere to lay his head. We prayerfully think of the countless numbers who sit down to hunger three times a day, of those who sleep rough, of young and not-so-young people who have opted out of life's mainstream. We think also of those who languish in prison, albeit through their own fault. We pray with eyes closed, but please help us to keep our eyes open for those crossing our paths whom we may be able to help. Accept the gifts which we offer in response to various appeals, that they may help just a little.

We rejoice at this season for the star of hope rising over the world's sorrows, who is Jesus Christ our Lord, and in whose name we offer our prayer.

263

As shepherds and rulers knelt before the cradle of the cosmic Christ, we bow before you, our God and our King.

We bow acknowledging your holiness and your lordship over all the kingdoms of this world.

In power and beauty you fashioned us for your glory, and for fellowship with you. You made us like yourself — creative, loving, good. But our sin broke that intimate fellowship for which we were born. We have groaned in our 'lostness', have helplessly tried to pull the threads of our lives into some meaningful pattern. But we were without hope until in your great grace you split the forces of darkness, and burst upon our world in light and love.

Our humble expressions of gratitude seem so paltry in the light of the gift which we contemplate today. We give to you all honour and praise and love, and we ask that as we come before you today, we shall be touched with a renewed sense of your glory. We pray that we shall rise from worship with the light of God, your light, so flaming in our hearts that we shall carry its warmth and brilliance into a world darkened by sin.

'Even so, come, Lord Jesus'. There is room in our hearts for you.

The Christmas season

264

Call to worship

John 1:14

God's logos made flesh!
Never before such wonder
Within time and space.

Dwelling among us,
Past belief in its flowering,
The hearing, touching.

And what the eyes see:
Ways and works all rich in grace
And human splendour,

Good in God's goodness,
Beautiful in his beauty
His image bearing.

Love is his language,
Reality revealing,
Earth's hopes fulfilling.

Thanks be to God!

265

Great God of the universe, we come into your presence
acknowledging that with our finite minds we can scarcely
comprehend that you chose to come and live among us for
a while, clothing yourself in our human frailty, and
revealing yourself to us in the person of Jesus.

Yet we thank you for the Christmas season, woven into the
Christian season long before it was taken over and
commercialised by the shops in the High Street and the
stores in the shopping malls. It affords us an opportunity to
reflect yet again upon your gift that has been so aptly
described as 'beyond words', to increase our understanding, and to relate that gift to the circumstances of our
lives.

As our minds travel through the events of the Christmas
story again this year, help our reflections to become so

deep that we can truly identify with those who were involved, and in that identification to see how you still relate to the deepest longings of our hearts.

May we find in the faith expressed by Mary and Joseph at the reception of the news, encouragement to believe that you can and do work for our good in all the situations of our lives, even those that come to us as a shock, and which leave us not quite the same as before.

May the inclusion in the story of people like Zechariah and Elizabeth prompt us to keep on praying even for seemingly hopeless situations, and then be ready for your answer.

May the record of the shepherds increase our awareness that you reveal yourself to us in the workplace just as much as in the worship-place, if only we have eyes to see and hearts willing to obey.

May the risks taken by the wise men, who left behind the safe and familiar to follow the light of truth, inspire us to move beyond our comfort zones when we sense that you are beckoning us to follow you along what are still uncharted ways.

May Simeon and Anna bring the assurance, especially to those of us who are aged or lonely or grieving, that we too can find in Jesus Christ this Christmastide our source of consolation, our fountain of hope, and our well of thanksgiving.

Grant us, we pray, the ability so to put ourselves in the picture, no matter what the circumstances of our lives, that we may find ourselves on Christmas morning kneeling in praise and adoration at the the feet of the One born to be King of kings and Lord of lords. In his name we pray.

266

Lord Jesus, as we look at the silver star marking the place where you were born, and see the manger where you lay as a babe, we see also the shadow of a cross over them. We know there can be no cross without the manger, but you knew there would be no manger without the cross.

Help us, Jesus, this Christmas, to remember that in our lives there is no birth without the pain and suffering of the Good Friday cross. Help us to bear that affliction in your name, and to know that there is a glorious Easter Resurrection after the cross.

Lord, implant these three images — the cradle, the cross and the empty tomb — vividly in our minds, so that we shall never forget the true meaning of Christmas, the true meaning your birth had for you and now for us.

Reconcile us to the Father, so that we may know the full joy of your salvation, and the glory of a life resurrected in and through you.

May all honour, glory and power be to your name, now and for ever.

267

O Christ of Christmas, would that we might have joined our voices with those of the angels who announced your advent.

Would that we might have followed the star of Bethlehem to kneel before your rough, rude birthplace.

But we are no less in awe of your majesty; we are no less grateful for your love.

And so, send us on our various ways to share the good news of your love, in your name.

268

Our Lord, Creator of light, we praise you for dividing the light from the darkness at the dawn of creation.

At this festive time of the year, we pray that your light will shine into our lives, dispelling the darkness of sin and greed and distrust.

Brighten our lives with the light of your love.

We thank you, Lord, for the marvellous, mystical spirit of Christmas. As we thrill to the sights and sounds of the season, help us to see beyond the bright lights and shimmering tinsel, and be aware of the darkness of despair in which so many of our neighbours live.

In the midst of the carol singing and season's greetings, may we hear the heart-cry of the needy.

Help us to do our part to brighten the dark places of our community and ease the anguish of our hurting neighbours.

We pray in the name of the Christ of Christmas, who said, 'I am come a light into the world'.

269

Our Lord, with the approach of Christmas, so many of us are filled with joyful anticipation. We listen for the sounds of Christmas, and long to hear children's laughter, Christmas music, silver bells, handbells, sleighbells. But these lovely sounds turn to cacophony as we hear other sounds of Christmas:

The anguished cry of the homeless, the pitiful cry of hungry children; the despairing voice of those with serious illness, the helpless voice of alcoholics and addicts.

Oh, Lord, help us to keep on doing what we can to bring harmony out of discord.

We want to say a prayer for those who are not all that excited about the arrival of Christmas:

those for whom there are financial problems, who will be unable to meet their family's expectations; those also who have no family, and whose loneliness will be deepened as they watch happy couples and family groups in yuletide celebrations; and those without homes.

May the true meaning of Christmas, which really has little to do with presents and parties, break through, and may those for whom we pray be cheered and strengthened by the realisation that Jesus came to earth just as surely for them as for anyone else.

We pray in the name of Christ, the author of miracles.

270

Lord, for many people Christmas is crazy — a season of hustle and hassle and hype. Help us all to rediscover the simplicity of the season, and the calm joy of the baby born at Bethlehem.

For some, Christmas is the loneliest time of the year — a reminder of happier days and loved ones now departed. O come, Immanuel, and make your presence felt in lonely lives.

Too often, Christmas means anything except what it is really all about — the birth of the one who can save us from ourselves, our foolishness and our pride.

Dear Father, help us to focus on him, on you, and on your needy children everywhere.

271

Our Lord God, author of all love, and source of all joy, we thank you for the happiness we have known during the days of Christmas. We thank you for the renewed links with family and friends, for overflowing human kindness, for gifts received and gladly given. Above all, we thank you for the strengthening of our faith that 'unto us a child is born, unto us a son is given', in whose name we come to pray and offer the thanksgiving of our hearts.

We thank you, O Father, that not only the eyes of simple shepherds looked on the infant Christ, but also that

> When wise men came seeking for Jesus from far,
> With rich gifts to greet him — and led by a star,
> They found in a stable the Saviour of men,
> A manger his cradle, so poor was he then.

Help us each as we make the same spiritual journey, and bless us all with the same spiritual discovery.

As we set our steps to the new year, may we go into the unknown with our hands in yours, knowing that this will be better than light and safer than a known way. May that almighty hand guide and uphold us each one, now and for ever.

272

Lord, we come in prayer like the shepherds and wise men of old, in wonder and adoration. We come to adore you, Christ the King.

In a world so stained and corrupted by commercialism and greed, we pause just now, and contemplate the wonder and generosity of the gift of love that Christmas signifies. Lord, keep us from a plastic and artificial Christmas spirit; keep our hearts and minds attuned to the wonder, joy and adoration which so marked that first Christmas.

Help us, O Lord, not to be so busy about the festivities, and the observance of ritual and tradition, that we miss the message and the true meaning of the baby in the manger.

Help us to realise, in all our celebrations and festivities this Christmas, that you gave the greatest gift, the gift of your own life, so that we might have salvation and reconciliation with God. In accepting that gift, may we know through the relationship which you made possible, true inner peace; and may we have goodwill to all people.

Help us not to supplant Christ with Christmas trees, true joys with frivolity, true peace with synthetic serenity. Help us, O Lord, to understand and to comprehend that you are indeed the Prince of Peace, the Wonderful Counsellor, the

Eternal Father. We pray that in all our celebrating this Christmas we may, above all, bow down in adoration before the King of kings.

273

Christ, our Immanuel,
God who became wrapped in human flesh
in the mighty miracle of your advent,

Let not our hearts this season
be as busy inns
with no room for your coming;

But help us to see
beyond the trimmings
and trappings of Christmas,
its true treasure —

Your infinite gift of love,
salvation, and life eternal.

Help us to celebrate your coming
with abundant joy,

and so to love and work
that your second coming
will likewise find us rejoicing,
to welcome, not a stranger,
but One long known and loved.

Because you were born —
not only in Bethlehem's manger,
but also in the cradle of our hearts.

The new year

274

At the threshold of a new year, O Father, we come to you in the name of Jesus, the Alpha and the Omega, the beginning and the end of all things. We thank you that in our times of change we can find in him one who never changes, whose love, mercy and grace are without end.

We give you thanks, Lord, for the year that is past:

for its joys which have enriched us;
for its disappointments which have enlightened us;
for its victories which have encouraged us;
and for its defeats which have strengthened us.

Forgive us, we pray, for those times when we failed to take hold of opportunities for service, for those times when we were guilty of forgetting you, for those times when we actually sinned. May we walk more closely with you in the year which lies ahead, so that we might serve you more worthily, and allow the beauty of Christ to be more clearly seen in our lives.

As we enter this new year, Father, we do so in faith, and pray that we shall journey in confidence, knowing that the Christ of the human road will be our constant companion in the way. May we be guided in all our decisions by the gracious light of your Holy Spirit.

275

O God, our Father, we approach this Lenten season of the year with awe and with wonder, and yet with desolation, as we walk with Christ in the desert place.

When we are tempted to feel that life is being hard upon us, let us remember our Lord's forty days of fasting and prayer. Bring to our recollection the torments which were set before him, and the sense of isolation and desperation that were his. And let us know again that the hardship was borne by him out of choice, so that he might understand the afflictions of those whose burdens he came to share.

Loving Father, during this holy time of year, let us journey in our hearts with Jesus in his onward walk to Gethsemane. Let us kneel with him in the garden, and stand with him at the place of trial. Give us courage to move with our Lord to Calvary, and to climb the mount by his side. Let us, we pray, be found in penitence at the foot of the cross.

More than this, Father, we cannot ask, for we know that we cannot share a place with him at the place of his dying; for, 'There was no other good enough to pay the price of sin.'

In this season, dear Lord, help us to search our hearts in the light of Christ's redeeming love. May our acts of self-denial be an echo of his ultimate sacrifice; and may our love for all men be motivated and nourished by the love which first loved us.

Palm Sunday

276

O God, our loving Father, on this Palm Sunday we gather in the name of the lowly Jesus, your Son. On this day we recall that he entered Jerusalem, the King coming to his own.

The world would have had him riding in triumph, leading a mighty army. In your word, Father, we read that he sat upon a borrowed donkey, and that those who followed him were a crowd of very ordinary people. We hear their cries of 'Hosanna', and we join our voices to theirs. But, O God, we know because we can look back, that many of those who acclaimed him as King so soon rejected him, mocked him, crucified him. Make us aware, we pray, of how easily we can be led from loyalty to denial, from commitment to indifference. The voices of the world are so strong, and we are so often afraid to be a small voice speaking out for Jesus, the gentle King.

On that first Palm Sunday, Father, your Son wept as he approached Jerusalem. We know only too well that he still weeps as he sees what we have done and what we have failed to do in his world. There is injustice and intolerance; war and aggression; greed and envy and selfishness and smugness; children are hungry and women weep and men live in fear of one another. The world is waiting for its King, its Light, its only Saviour. May it know him when he comes!

Today, yet again, may we with the angels 'Look down with sad and wondering eyes to see the approaching sacrifice.'

277

O God, our Father, we remember on this Palm Sunday how our Lord and Saviour, Jesus Christ, moved with courage into the arena where his obedience to your righteous will would be seen to be done.

We blend our voices with the acclamation of those crowds who thronged the road into the city of Jerusalem. More than that, we trust in Christ as the Saviour of the world, who for our sakes turned not from the cross, but drained its bitter cup of agony and shame to the end, with conviction, joy and in gladness.

We call him Lord, and in his name we worship you as truly one God, Creator, Redeemer and sanctifying Spirit.

Holy week

278

Our heavenly Father,
we thank you for this holy week
and its sacred meaning for us,
as we commemorate the Passion
and the victory of our Lord
that has brought to us
salvation, joy and life eternal.

Give to us a deeper revelation
of your divine love,

sublimely expressed on Calvary,
and lead us to a greater commitment
to do your will and work.

We praise you that this week
does not end with Good Friday,
but with Easter Sunday;
not with a defeat,
but with a victory;
not with a crucifixion,
but with a coronation.

Fill our souls once again
with the hope and joy
of a resurrection faith,
and with your radiant presence
on our pathway of life.

Good Friday

279

Lord Christ, we feel the pain and shame of your crucifixion. That men and women could look upon your glory;
be aware of your love; benefit from your teaching and
miracles; and yet decide to crucify you appals us. What
evil forces are at work in human hearts!

This day reminds us of the depth of human sin and lets us
glimpse the depth of your great love. Thank you for
accepting Calvary. Our hearts are moved by your refusal

217

to come down from the cross by some dramatic display of power, because we know that your suffering not only revealed your love, but enabled us to be forgiven.

On this special day of remembrance, we ask that you will burn into our minds and hearts the cost of our salvation. Help us to value even more all you have done for us, and be even more determined not to sin, because our sin will cause you to suffer more.

Today, tenderly and persuasively, draw us to your cross, and let us see your glory there.

280

Eternal God, who in your love gave your Son to the death of the cross for our salvation; who by your mighty power delivered him from the grave for our victory over death; who by his glorious resurrection brought us into an inheritance eternal and incorruptible; enable us by your Holy Spirit to die daily to sin, that we may evermore live as people of the resurrection, knowing that the things which are seen are temporal, but the things which are not seen are eternal. Through Jesus Christ, our risen Lord.

281

Heavenly Father, we meet to remember the day of the death of your Son, our brother, Jesus Christ. We come, not to celebrate his crucifixion, but rather to contemplate the significance of the deeds of this dark day.

Why have we called it *Good* Friday? Do we try to temper the terror with a tender word like 'good'?

God of our salvation, help us to understand our relationship to the cross. To know that Christ died for our sins. That we are sinners, saved by your grace alone.

Grant us to understand the meaning of the words of the apostle Paul, who wrote of 'being crucified with Christ', and of what it means to be 'dead in trespasses and sins'. Let us feel the results of Christ's words from the cross: 'Father, forgive them'. Let us know what it is to be alive in Christ.

Bring to this day of mixed emotions the calming assurance of your peace which passes all understanding. May the remembrance of Calvary bring hope, regardless of what we might call this day.

We pray in the name of our crucified Lord and risen Saviour, Jesus Christ.

282

O Lord our God, we come before you with great reverence, to acknowledge your infinite love to the world in the giving of your only Son as an atonement for sin.

This visible expression of yourself is beyond our comprehension, yet we open our hearts and lives in faith, claiming the pardon you offer at such great cost.

How we thank you for Jesus, who not only showed us how to live, but in his humiliation and pain enfolded us all in his suffering and death. For us he has broken the power of sin and Satan, bringing us into the light and freedom of your great grace. Father, we accept by faith that finished work, and offer ourselves in gratitude and praise. In him, we are accepted as your sons and daughters, children of the heavenly Kingdom of the redeemed.

Accept us as we humbly worship, and help us to understand still further the mystery of redemption.

As we reflect on the wonder of Calvary, help us to bring every thought into captivity, pondering in our hearts its eternal challenge.

Lord, make Calvary real to us. We pray in the name of Jesus our Saviour, King and Lord for ever.

283

Our loving heavenly Father, it is only by your great grace that we feel able to enter into your presence, and dare to speak your name.

The immense sacrifice made on our behalf by Jesus is more real than ever. We are again reminded of your love. Though we are sinful, we praise and thank you for the means to escape, for ever, from our shackles of sin!

We thank you for your Holy Spirit, who has again brought to remembrance our objective — to be more like Jesus. In some meaningful way, we want to reveal his life through ours.

So, Lord, we present ourselves to you. Some of us here need forgiveness of sin, and we thank you that Calvary's sacrifice is still redemptive. Please free the heart that is broken by sin; the mind that is warped by the debasement of the world around us. Bring forgiveness, healing and wholeness.

Some of us seek renewal. We are reminded that our living and our service ought to be and can be better. We love you, and we want to be fully available for your use.

Come, Holy Spirit, and deeply cleanse. Fill us with yourself. Take away even the desire and tendency to sin. Make us clean, pure, a place where you are comfortable in taking up residence.

Thank you for the reminder that all of these blessings are possible, and can be ours because of Christ. We celebrate all that you are, and now give ourselves wholly to you.

Accept our humble and earnest prayer, for we seek you, O God, in the name of our Lord who is yet alive!

Easter Sunday

284

Triumphant Christ, thank you for allowing all who believe in you to share in your resurrection victory. We praise you for destroying for ever the power of death, and for releasing health and goodness and gladness into our dying world.

O Saviour, we tremble at the sight of your wounds which were made for our salvation. We are transfixed at your risen glory, through which we have eternal life.

Thank you for being the hope of the world. Thank you for releasing captives. Thank you for rising to new life in all your splendour. And thank you that we are alive — radiantly alive — in you.

Dear victorious Christ, we live in the light of your triumph, and we sing 'Hallelujah' on this Easter morning!

These praises we bring in the power of the Holy Spirit.

285

O God our Father, we praise you for sending your Son Jesus to bless the people of his age, and to be our teacher, and give us an example of good living for all time. We praise you much more for the salvation that comes to us through his sacrifice on the cross. We confess and repent of our sin, and claim by faith the salvation offered by our crucified Lord.

On this Easter Day, we rejoice above all that he rose from the dead, giving us the assurance of eternal life.

Hallelujah, Christ arose!

We thank you, Lord Jesus, for those who shared your earthly life, and we pray that the glory of the Easter story may not be lost on us today. Help us to know:

the joy of Mary, who went to embalm a corpse and met
a living Lord;
the joy of Peter and John who were lamenting the loss
of a dear friend, but who met a Saviour who
would always be near to them and real to them;
the joy of the two who on the walk from Jerusalem to
Emmaus were grieving over dashed hopes, but
who found an eternal presence;
the joy of Thomas whose doubts were overwhelmed by
the certainty of faith.

May we all today know the presence of that risen Christ,
and the joy that comes when he is near.

Lord of our lives, we pray that you will guide us into ways
of spreading the news of your resurrection power. Help us
to evidence it in our own lives, and to bring the truth of
your triumph over death to those entombed in sin, that
they may in faith break free.

May the resurrection message come with hope of eternity
to those who are persecuted for righteousness' sake; to
those who are kept low by illness; to those who are limited
by handicap; to those whose relationships have turned
sour. May they all be empowered to endure, in the
knowledge that the worst that can be hurled against us in
this life can be transformed in the beauty of the life to
come.

As your disciples waited the coming of your Spirit at
Pentecost, so we wait in this time of worship to be filled
with the power of your Spirit, to be cleansed by the purity
of your Spirit, to be given vision by the revelations of your
Spirit.

All these things we pray in the name of our crucified, risen and glorified Lord, and for the sake of his Kingdom here and hereafter.

Ascension Day

286

Lord Jesus Christ, conqueror of death and giver of life, we thank you for the benefits inherited by your Church through your ascension into Heaven.

You promised that if you went away, the Holy Spirit would be sent. We long to receive the blessings he offers; to take possession of the gifts he bestows; and, in our lives, produce the fruit of his indwelling.

Your word declares that when we have sinned you are the one who speaks to God our Father in our defence. Thank you for pleading on our behalf. In accordance with your prayers, may we be one in you in heart and mind.

Thank you for the promise of your presence. By the merits of your suffering and death, you have been given the supreme place of honour in Heaven. Yet, freed from the limitations of the flesh you still desire to be with us — invisible, but everywhere available. O disclose yourself to us in all your majesty and humility!

Thank you for the affirmation given by the two unnamed men at your ascension who said that you will come again in a similar manner to your departure. Make us ready and worthy to be received by you on that glorious day.

Pentecost

287

O God, sustainer and sanctifier of all your creation, we praise you on this day for the promise which has been fulfilled in our midst: the coming to Christ's people of the Holy Spirit. We thank you for the life and teaching of Jesus whilst upon earth in his bodily presence; and we thank you on this Pentecost Day that his exhortations to holy living are made possible to us in the power of his eternal Spirit.

We turn our minds back to that first Pentecost after our Lord's death, and we recall, O God, that the fire of the Holy Spirit came amongst *all* the people, and yet it sat upon the heads of *each one*. As a congregation in this place today, we pray that your Spirit shall again manifest himself to us all, but shall make his dwelling with and within each of us.

God of power, fill us with your powerful Spirit. God of peace, fill us with your peaceful Spirit. God of cleansing, fill us with your cleansing Spirit. God of holiness, fill us with your Holy Spirit.

These prayers we offer for ourselves, and for all the people of Christ's church on earth. In the name of our risen and glorified Lord.

288

Almighty God, we hear the call to prayer and worship, and gladly we respond. We acknowledge you to be eternally creator and sustainer of life. We trust in and believe the holy gospel, that in Jesus Christ your Son you came in physical and bodily form to redeem the world you had created, and that in his broken body we may perceive your heart of love. In his Easter triumph we see your victory over sin and death.

We meet on this day and remember that at Pentecost you came again into our world in spiritual power, confirming for ever the redemptive work of Christ. On this day and in this place we number ourselves with that company of men and women long ago who first received your Holy Spirit as an obedient and prayerful community. We meet as Christian believers today, members of Christ's church on earth, which through the ages has experienced the sustaining and sanctifying fellowship of the Holy Spirit.

Almighty God, we worship you in the name of Christ, and by the aid of the same Holy Spirit, with humble yet uplifted hearts.

Harvest

289

Almighty God, it is from your unfailing store of goodness, both spiritual and material, that we draw our strength. In our times of pride and boasting, let us ever remember that this is so. Keep us always aware that our advances in technology result only from discovering those resources which you have already provided, and that we can create no new thing.

At this time of harvest celebration, we who are gathered together praise you for sustaining us in body from the fruits of the earth. Our needs are more than met from the gifts which your good hand has supplied. For another harvest, safely gathered in, we give you thanks. We thank you also for the hands of those who have laboured on our behalf, bringing forth the earth's riches. May we never take for granted the meals which are set before us, day after day, but rather let us use them as a sacrament of praise, and an opportunity of recognising your goodness.

As we rejoice in our abundance, O Lord, let us keep in our minds and hearts those for whom there has been a failed harvest; those for whom the economics of their nation mean that many go hungry and starve. It would be so easy for us to blame you for the geography and the climate and other natural conditions which affect those lands. And yet we know that the needs of all who go without can be met from the fulness of those who have too much. Give us, then, a practical compassion for the hungry. Grant us the wisdom and the unselfishness to bring our rich resources to starving children and grieving parents. As we sing our harvest praise, O Lord, may we in the depths of our hearts weep with those who weep.

We pray that again at this time of year, we shall be reminded of the spiritual harvest to which Jesus turned the eyes of his followers. May we be kept ever mindful that our calling as your people is to gather souls into the harvest of the Kingdom. In the name of our Saviour we pray.

290

Eternal God, our Father, we remember your promise that while the earth remains, seedtime and harvest, cold and heat, summer and winter, day and night shall not cease.

We give thanks that your promise remains, and that the earth continues to give seed to the sower, and bread to the eater, through waving fields of wheat and golden grain.

Father, give us wisdom to protect and to nurture the earth, that future generations might be nourished by her bounty.

We give thanks for the world and its beauty — for the landscape and the seascape, for the mists on the mountains and the wonder of the stars. We hear the song of birds, and see the beauty of flowers, and we give you praise.

We who live in homes that you have provided for us give thanks for them, and for our fellow men, for friends whom we love and who love us, for the laughter of children and the joy of family relationships.

We thank you for the manifold joys of harvest, and we ask that when we each are gathered to the eternal world, the fruits of our lives may be pleasing to you — the Lord of harvest home.

Hear the prayers of your people, as we pray in the name of him who brought us to you.

291

O God, the creator of all things,
you have filled the world with beauty.
Open our eyes that we might see you in your creation.

We are thankful for the awesome resources
you have entrusted to us,
and we are ashamed that we sometimes misuse them.
Forgive us our foolishness, and teach us to be faithful
stewards.

We are especially thankful for the blessings of this harvest.
We receive these gifts of grain and fruit and nature's
bounty
with grateful hearts and open hands.

Give us wisdom,
that we might neither squander nor hoard the perfect gifts
that come to us through your mercy and love.

Through Jesus Christ, your Son and our Lord.

Mothering Sunday (Mothers' Day)

292

Our heavenly Father, this day is special for you, because it was you who 'invented' families, and gave to mothers a special place in your purposes.

As families celebrate together today, may their appreciation of mothers and motherhood be bright with thanksgiving to you, the giver of all good gifts. And may children of all ages learn to express their love in words and deeds through the privileged years when mothers are with them.

Please, Lord, make this worship time an oasis of encouragement for mothers who are anxious about their children — about a behaviour problem, an unhelpful friendship, a health concern. Reassure mothers who have members of family away from home — studying, or working, or bringing up families of their own. May they be mindful to keep in touch, and may parents learn to be caring without being possessive, and without recriminations when replies to letters from home are a long time coming.

As you are the God who cares for the fatherless and the widow, we remember before you the lone parents, whose family responsibilities and financial burdens are often frighteningly heavy. May they never be allowed to feel left out or misunderstood in the family fellowship of your people.

Accept our thanks for all the adoptive mothers and foster-mothers who give love and security to children deprived of home life with their natural parents.

Surround with your loving-kindness, Father, any who would dearly love children of their own, and have so far been denied them. You understand how their faith is tested in this gathering of parents and children.

Because you have set the solitary in families, Lord, make this truly a day of sharing, of including people who would otherwise be on their own. May we allow no one to feel alone in our company. Make this a day of updating our relationships, through the challenge of this time of family worship. Make us eager to believe in one another, and to bring out the best in one another. Set our hearts aglow in the warmth of your love.

All this we pray in the name of Jesus our Saviour, who taught us to be considerate and unselfish in our loving.

293

Loving God, today we thank you for those who have always 'been there' for us.

Thank you for the happy experiences of acceptance, and love, and nurture that have made it easy for us to trust you as our loving God.

Thank you especially for mothers whose faithful and unselfish loving has enriched our lives.

We do know, of course, Lord, that for some the celebration and togetherness of today awakens painful memories, or feelings of loss and loneliness.

Oh, God, help us most of all this day to honour your unfailing and steadfast love, and to recognise that we are all members of your family.

Help us to share one another's joy and pain, and to realise that you are the one who is there for all of us.

294

Dear Father, we are glad that our calendar has a Mothers' Day. As your own life demonstrated, mothers are meant to be special people.

You chose an ordinary woman, Mary, for an extraordinary role, yet without question she accepted this from you. We who are mothers identify with Mary, 'keeping all manner of things, and pondering them in our hearts'. Mothers' hearts are so accommodating — sharing cares, disappointments, hurts, hopes and joys.

Give us a Mary-heart, Father, not only for our own children, but for those who look to us for a mother-voice, a mother-hand, a mother-smile and a mother-heart. As Mary pointed others to Jesus, knowing he was not only hers but yours, use us as mothers to be channels to lead others to Jesus.

You do us honour, Father, and we praise you.

295

Almighty God and loving heavenly Father, we come before you in the ever-blessed name of Jesus, on this 'All the World' Sunday.

In your sight, O Lord, our world is only a very small sphere in the great universe you have created. Yet, Lord, its population is so large and its problems are so immense. Forgive us, Lord, when we divide your world and separate its peoples.

Whatever their race, all human beings are created in your divine image, and kept within your loving care.

Thank you, Lord, for providing this day, when we can cast our minds beyond concerns of our immediate locality, a day when we may try to see our world as you see it, hear the cries of the needy as you hear them, perceive the inequalities and injustices as you perceive them, and sense the burdens of the nations which you bear.

Lord, today may your Holy Spirit enlighten us, challenge us, and certainly inspire us, so that we may more effectively take our place in your world and serve others to the best of our ability.

We praise you, Lord, that you raised up your Church to stretch its arms of compassion around 'all the world'. The church universal lifts up the saving name of Jesus. Be pleased, Lord, to own and bless the ministry of your messengers in every country where the gospel is made known. As your word is proclaimed, may many receive your salvation and experience new life in Christ.

Bring peace, Lord, where there is conflict, unity where there is division, and understanding where there is disagreement.

O Lord, in this world of need, some face starvation through drought or war. We plead for an end to the drought and peace where there is strife. In praying this way, Lord, we recognise that in all the world there are far more needs than we can bring to you in these brief moments of intercession. Interpret, O Lord, the desires that arise in our hearts for our brothers and sisters both far and near. Our prayers we present in the name of Jesus, the world's Saviour.

296

Lord, you told us not to be anxious.
Yet we are!
Anxious for all those uprooted from their homes and
country
through the meaningless destruction of war.
'Innocents' of our time — young and old;
victims of man's continuing inhumanity to man.

(Response)

Lord, be with them!

We feel so helpless, not knowing what to do.
Yet we hear you calling us to hope and not despair;
to reach out beyond our limitations

into a future that will be
a new beginning.
Help us then to see you, Lord,
suffering with them and for them,
a brother in anxiety
and living source of hope,
from whom new time, potentiality and freedom
will continue to flow.

(Response)

Thanks be to God!

Christ, we look to you,
asking your help and intervention.
Move in mercy among them in your Spirit,
empowering all who serve their needs,
guiding all who seek and plan for peace,
and in your wisdom,
admonishing those who would despoil it.

(Response)

Lord, hear our prayer!

297

Father God, we realise at this moment in our world's
history how much we need your guidance, your strength
and your wisdom. The world's leaders face problems and
decision-making far beyond themselves, and we long for a
higher wisdom to fall upon them.

We pray that those in positions of power and responsibility
may understand that the lives of people and nations lie in

their hands. May they be enlightened to the weight of their responsibilities. Give them the courage and honesty and moral integrity to confess their need of wisdom from you. Only then can they ever hope to lead the nations of this world down paths of peace.

For ourselves, remind us, O Lord, that 'A mighty fortress is our God' — not a hiding place, where we can hide from life's tough decisions, but rather a storehouse of courage and of strength.

May your arms, love and comfort surround us all, and may we find refuge under your wings, Almighty God.

298

Forgive us, Lord —

We have become so used to them now, those images of wide-eyed children, ribs protruding, bellies distended; starving families ravaged by war or famine or disease. The images flicker across our television screens and across our minds. They form an ironic contrast with the stream of advertisements that flood our screens and our minds. Each of them insisting upon our need for bigger, better and brighter products.

Forgive us, Lord —

For being so easily lulled into comfort and unconcern, content to be cocooned from the reality of what is happening to our brothers and sisters, your children, children of the 'inasmuch' God.

Forgive us, Lord —

Help us to do better, to give better, to care better, to pray better . . . aware that as we seek your face we find that it is turned towards these your children with love and compassion.

Turn your face upon them Lord.

Grant them an awareness of your love, and help us to work in your strength to establish their well-being and peace. For their sake, and for Jesus' sake.

299

Heavenly Father,
who gave your only Son
for the salvation of the whole world,
save us from being individual islands of life,
untouched by divine commandment and human need.

Enlarge our vision,
expand our boundaries of concern,
extend our hands of caring
to those who need the touch of love.

Change our mirrors into windows
that we may see beyond ourselves
to the hurts and heartaches
of those in trial and in tragedy.

Help us to weigh our necessities
against the needs of others.

Save us from waste and from
being overfed in a hungry world.

Extend our hands of caring
to bring the bread of sustenance
to those who suffer hunger of the body,
and the bread of life to those
in spiritual want and need.

Let the light of your love and truth
govern our thoughts and guide our hands,
that we might be channels of your redeeming love
to our troubled and tortured world.

A new academic year

300

Dear Father, we come with our prayers on this day, which
stands at the eve of a new year for so many young people.
In our prayers, we remember and ask your blessing upon
those for whom the next few days will see a return to
academic life.

Some of our little ones will be starting proper school for
the first time ever. They will be excited, but anxious, and
we know that the tears may flow. Watch over and guard
each one, we pray, and keep them safe.

For some, there will be a change from junior school to senior school. We think of them and pray for them, as they move into perhaps a rougher and more crowded environment. Help us all to be careful for them, and to share in their new experiences through our interest.

To those who are entering a year of major examinations, we ask that you will give clear minds. Help them to lean upon you in times of stress, but at the same time let them know that there are so many who are willing to be there for them — teachers, parents, Christian friends, counsellors.

We pray especially for those who will be going to their first year at college or university. This will be so different for them, Lord, from anything they have previously known. The academic demands will be greater, and separation from family and home will bring its challenges. There will be pressures and times of self-doubt. We ask, O Lord, that our young people will quickly learn a calm dependence upon your grace. Give to them, we pray, fellowship with others in the faith, who will be a source of spiritual and practical support. And may we in this congregation also be supportive of them in whatever way we can.

May your blessing be upon all Christian teachers, lecturers and tutors. We ask that they will be keenly conscious of the privileges and obligations which are theirs, as they have responsibility for moulding the minds and lives of so many.

Our prayers we offer in the name of Jesus, the great teacher.

301

Dear God, it is good to come into your house today, and to be in the company of other Christians.

We have set aside this day to consider the ministry of healing, through those whom you have chosen to be instruments of your power. We thank you for them, for their training, for their expertise. We thank you for their concern for the needs of others. We know that when illness, tragedy and other life-changing events take place, we can turn to such people for help. May we not take for granted the constancy of your intervention in our lives through other folk.

We thank you for all these trained representatives of healing. Continue to empower and strengthen them in their work, and grant that they in turn will look to you, remembering that you are their source of skill.

We know, Lord, that pain, pressures, grief and loss can also provide us with opportunity to flex our spiritual muscles. Let us not forget that you can be the source of all our inner strength and confidence, and the ultimate answer to the problems we face in life.

Thank you, Lord, that you can meet all our needs. Thank you that you can be the key to our wholeness. Help us to turn over to you the pressures and stresses that we experience. Teach us to relax in your Spirit.

May the same Holy Spirit be with us now, as we listen. Help us to grow spiritually, and to become what you want us to be. Hear us in our prayers.

O God, our loving Father, we come to you in a spirit of praise, to thank you for your wonderful gift of medical science. We pray for all scientists who are on the frontiers of new discoveries. May they pursue that which is best for your world, that which brings about humankind's greater good within your purposes.

We thank you for the gift of healing. Your power is beyond our understanding. You choose at times to manifest your glory and bring healing without human help, but we humbly acknowledge that mostly you entrust your healing work to people, whom you equip with knowledge and skill. We thank you for all in the world who are used as your agents in this way, whether they recognise this fact or not.

In particular, dear Father, we pray for members of our own congregation who meet in your presence now — those whom you have blessed with medical knowledge in their own field of expertise. We thank you for the skills they have acquired and developed as they have practised their profession. They witness to a sense of privilege that in partnership with you, they continue your ongoing healing work in the world. We thank you for them all — those who diagnose, prescribe and give treatment; those who operate, who care, who counsel, who pray and who give practical support. We acknowledge the ability of those who administer and who provide a lovely environment for those who are ill.

Strengthen them all by your grace, as they minister daily to medical, emotional and spiritual needs. Give them, we ask, all the personal resources they need when they are tired or under stress themselves. May the Spirit of Jesus who is love and compassion be theirs, and enable them at these difficult times.

Grant them all a renewed sense of being involved with you in the ministry of healing. In the name of Jesus we pray.

Remembrance Sunday

303

We stand hesitantly and humbly in your presence on this day, Lord. We call it a day of remembrance, and yet there is so much that we would rather forget. But we dare not forget, for on this day of all days we recall shame at its most shameful and tragedy at its most tragic. To our memories once again is brought a picture of those who were made in your image destroying each others and themselves; those who should be brothers and sisters of Christ killing and wounding and torturing those others of your children. We cannot repent for those who have gone before us, Lord, but we confess that we in our own hearts have been guilty of the same feelings of envy and intolerance and greed which caused war to happen. Let us not be instigators of hatred and aggression for our own ends. And let us not forget the horrors of conflicts past, lest we be too easily persuaded to go that way again. Yet, we recognise also the nobility of spirit and valour of body which wars have so often brought forth, and we thank you for the courage of those upon whom our earthly freedom has historically depended.

We do right, O God, to remember those in this land and in this congregation who grieve as a result of armed conflict. The widows and the fatherless we bring before you, and those wounded in body and bitter in mind and spirit. Continue to work a work of healing in them. This day will again be a day of tears. Comfort the sorrowful, we pray. Let them take strength from the familiar words that those they loved 'shall grow not old, as we that are left grow old; age shall not weary them, nor the years condemn'.

Whilst we cannot glory in war, we do ask, O Lord, that we shall each be bold in resisting evil and oppression. Let us keep in our minds that as you are a God of peace, so also you are a God of justice. Our prayers of remembering, reflection and penitence we offer in the name of the crucified and risen Saviour of all men.

304

Father God, we come to you today in anxiety and apprehension concerning the affairs of the nations. Help us to realise that this is your world, and you are in it, above it, and beyond it. May we ever remember that you are not a spectator God, who watches indifferently the affairs of mankind. Remind us, O Lord, that you too once walked this earth, wounded and bleeding, knowing the agony of men.

We confess, Lord, that at moments like this, we feel so powerless and forsaken. Help us not to give way to hopelessness and despair. Prompt us to recall that you are still the King of kings, the creator and power behind the universe, and that you have a plan and destiny for your creation. We yearn for the day when your will shall be done on earth as it is in Heaven; when all nations shall know you; and every tongue confess that Jesus Christ is Lord.

Uphold us with the hope and encouragement that these prayers we utter will not be in vain; that no matter how dark and menacing the days ahead, you are still the light of the world.

We pray that the hearts and minds of world leaders will be opened to the guidance of your Spirit; that he, in his secret way, shall prevail where men have so pathetically failed. May your will be fulfilled.

Our entreaty we offer in Jesus' name.

Bible Sunday

305

O God our Father, you who are all-powerful and all-knowing, and who made all things, including man himself, we marvel that you should want to communicate with us, and should want to bless us by a plan for our salvation and for our progress in godliness.

We praise you that in the fulness of time you sent your Son, Jesus Christ our Lord, to be the vital communicator of your will for mankind.

And we give you thanks for the Scriptures of the Old and New Testaments which tell us of the gradual unfolding of your plan to your people, and for the expounding of your way of salvation and godliness which came to, and through, the early Church.

Help us to bring to our understanding of your word a similar sensitivity, and a like seeking after truth, which will bring us nearer to yourself and not further from our fellow human beings. Help us to use the Scriptures as a lamp for our feet and bread for spiritual hunger, rather than a rod for the backs of others.

We thank you for those who saw new light and pointed it out to their fellows. We thank you for those who wrote down the discoveries that they or others had made, and for all who preserved those writings so that we can read them today. We thank you for all who have translated your word into other languages and for those who have retranslated it into the speech of our day. We thank you for all who have commented upon it, that we might understand its messages better. And we thank you for all who have preached your word faithfully and clearly, often in the face of persecution and misunderstanding. Help us in our turn to interpret truly, and to proclaim fearlessly, what you have revealed to mankind.

We ask your blessing on all Bible societies, and others who are seeking to make the Scriptures more and more available to all nations of the world.

Help us not just to read your word and to understand it, but to live it, for the building up of ourselves in holiness, and for the enlightenment of all who may see an expression of yourself in us.

So teach us, Lord, to use each power
  As we the doctrine shall adorn,
That truth and grace shall spring to flower
  In lives renewed and souls reborn;
As we to all the world unfold
  The glory of the faith we hold.

306

Our Father, with the psalmist we pray, 'Open our eyes to behold wondrous things out of thy word'. We ask that your power shall be seen

  inspiring the writers of the written word;
    touching the readers of the read word;
      using the preachers of the spoken word;
        and sanctifying the hearers of the holy word.

For 'faith cometh by hearing, and hearing by the word of God'.

These prayers we bring in the name of Jesus Christ, the living Word of God made flesh.

307

Dear God and loving Father, in your goodness and tender mercy you have given us your priceless book, to be a light to our feet and a lamp upon our way. It is from the precious pages of the Bible that we learn of you, and of the glorious salvation which you have provided.

We thank you for this special Sunday, which reminds us of all the treasures of your word, and which inspires us to be more diligent in searching out those treasures. Without a knowledge of the Scriptures, O God, how can we know, receive and transmit those great truths which can lead to salvation? Turn our minds and thoughts, we pray, more faithfully to the study of the word of life.

As we look upon that word today with joy and thanksgiving, we are grateful for those whom you chose to write it down, and for those in our lifetime who are faithful in proclaiming it. And yet, Lord, no matter how important are these servants, none is greater than the treasures of truth which they deliver from your word. These truths are the rule by which we measure and judge the doctrines of our Christian faith.

We pray, O God, that you will make us careful in teaching the young, fervent in extending the gospel to those who do not know you, and trustworthy in our own reading and study of the holy word.

On this day, we once more commit ourselves with deep devotion to searching the Scriptures. In them may we find a daily renewal of our understanding of your will and the strength to do it with all our minds and hearts. In Jesus' name we pray.

308

O God, Father and ruler of us all, we meet on this Sunday to bring honour and glory to your word. We pray that all who proclaim it today may be filled with your power and love, so that in a radiant way your Kingdom may be blessed and your name glorified.

We all claim your continued help, that we might be more faithful in the ministry of your word. We recall the treasures you have given us in the Bible, and we want to share those treasures with those who dwell in the darkest corners of our world. Pour out your grace upon the spiritually needy everywhere. Make us all faithful messengers of the word, so that all people will have opportunity to increase in knowledge of your love and salvation.

Bless us and your word on this Bible Sunday, we pray. For your Kingdom's sake.

THE CHRISTIAN LIFE

For spiritual renewal

309

Lord, we want to be renewed by your Holy Spirit. We look to you and to you alone for this. We want to be renewed in your way. Help us not to look for short cuts. Direct us to your words.

So often, Lord, fear holds us back. Then we set up boundaries and are only prepared to go so far. Dear Father, help us to be willing to abandon ourselves completely to you, so that in your service we may be reckless, because we are prepared to pour out our lives for you.

Help us to remember that renewal by your Holy Spirit brings a freedom in the Holy Ghost. But, O Lord, remind us always that this freedom does not give us licence to do what we like.

We bow before you humbly just now. We confess our need. We desire your Holy Spirit to do his work now. In Jesus' name we ask our prayers.

310

O God, our Father, how often our spirits are dulled and desensitised to your presence and your power. We know all too well our hearts' need for times of refreshing — in our own spirits, and in this fellowship of your people. We long for your Spirit to fall upon us like gentle rain upon the dust, causing fresh shoots of green to break through the parched soil of our spirits with the promise of life.

You have said through your servant Isaiah, 'When the poor and needy seek water, and there is none, and their tongue is parched with thirst, I the Lord will answer them; I the God of Israel will not forsake them. I will open rivers on the bare heights, and fountains in the midst of the valleys; I will make the wilderness a pool of water, and the dry land springs of water . . . that men may see and know, may consider and understand together, that the hand of the Lord has done this'.

We *want* to claim your promise. Right now! But in honesty, Lord, we ask ourselves if we really want to take the risk of renewal. Perhaps it is just the sense of it which our jaded spirits crave — the stimulation, the reminder that after all we are loved. But the risk of renewal — the risk of what it might require of us, or where your vitalising Spirit might drive us — that is frightening, Lord. We are more comfortable in our mediocrity than we care to admit. Now we find ourselves praying that you will disturb us, by inundating us with a blessing we may not be able to contain, and cannot control. How can we know what that will mean? Your Spirit is not given by measure. Once released among us, there is no negotiating the outcomes. We know you well enough to know, Lord, that what begins as a gentle benediction showered upon us may issue in swift streams of cleansing grace sweeping unrestrained through our souls. Make us ready, then, for what you will do among us. Deliver us from a cautious faith, that cannot dare to think what might be should your grace be released to flow freely among us.

Come, Holy Spirit, refresh, renew! Cleanse our minds and our motives, so sullied by their exposure to the suffocating influences of the world about us. Increase our faith! Expand our vision! Inspire our devotion! And glorify yourself among us, so that a watching world will see and know that the hand of the Lord has done this.

In Jesus' all-availing name we pray.

311

Dear heavenly Father, you are so very patient with us, and so kind to us. We thank you for this.

So often, we have allowed our relationship with you to become strained, because we have failed in our seeking after the grace of thankfulness, especially when you have blessed us.

Dear God, we have ascribed the success you gave us to ourselves, and have not given you the praise, the glory and the honour. We seek your forgiveness, and ask that you will grant us the spirit of humility and meekness.

We humbly ask that you will renew our minds and our wills, so that we shall daily seek your guidance in all things. Through Jesus Christ our Lord.

312

Come, great Paraclete,
alongside to help us
with the business of living,

that we may be adequate
and counted faithful.

Come, mighty Comforter,
give us needed strength
for the testings of life,
and grant to us your peace
amid life's traumas and trials.

Come as the wind;
sweep away our doubts,
clear away the clutter,
invigorate our spirits
and refresh our souls.

Come as the fire;
cleanse and refine,
purify and purge,
kindle on the altar of our hearts
a flame of undying love.

Come as the seal;
stamp upon us
the likeness of our Lord,
the winsomeness of his love,
the beauty of his holiness.

Come, Holy Spirit,
make our hearts
your abiding place,
 and adorn them with all your
fruit and graces.

The Church — its unity and its ministry

313

Almighty God, we come into your presence, who are the one God and Father of us all. In our hearts we hear the words, 'One Lord, one faith, one baptism', and we thank you that these concepts are becoming more clearly understood and followed.

Let us remember, Lord, that the Church is yours and does not belong just to us and our friends. Help us not to covet a little bit of it for ourselves, and think that this is the only bit that matters, the only bit that you can be happy with, the only bit that is doing your work in your way.

We do thank you, Lord, for that expression of the Church where we have opportunity to worship and witness. We thank you for its triumphs of yesterday, its ministry of today, and its potential for tomorrow. You have owned our faith and our works, and we thank you humbly for doing so.

But we ask that you will let us look with approving eyes and speak with encouraging words when we see others worshipping Christ and practising their faith in ways different from our own. Help us to be numbered with those who strive for the reconciliation of his broken body on earth.

We pray just now for the worldwide proclamation of the gospel by pastors and priests, by curates and captains, by ministers and monks. We pray for the spiritual and practical ministry of so many whose only ordination is that of the Holy Spirit, and whose works and witness are a testimony to Christ throughout the earth. May all see that in essentials we are all one, as you, our Father, and your Son are One.

We thank you for the redeeming love by which we became members of your Church, the mystical body of Christ in the world. Let us never betray its fellowship, nor the honour of its Lord, in whose saving name we pray.

314

Heavenly Father, when your Son, our Saviour, prayed 'that they all may be one', the gospel record tells us that incredibly he was not only praying for his disciples, but for us who are present-day followers of Christ, for us who believe in him because of the witness of that first disciple band. We are to be one 'so that the world may believe'.

With shame and sadness, O God, we confess how far short we often fall in being one in love with others in your universal church. Small wonder that the world does not yet believe.

Because some Christians choose to worship you with swinging incense and tinkling bells, some with mighty organ music, some with hands upraised, and some with banners, bonnets and bands, we have allowed our petty prejudices to supersede our love for each other. The limitations of our own rut-thinking have lessened our usefulness to you.

You created your world with a vast variety of colours and creatures, so we cannot think you would want the worship of all of your churches to be stereotyped. But we confess that we sometimes allow our own preferences to isolate us from each other, even to thinking more highly than we ought of our own ways.

Place within our hearts, O God, a love that will transcend all denominational barriers; a love that cares more for the building of your Kingdom than for man-made traditions; a love that binds all believers into a mighty Christian army which, though made up of many regiments, marches unitedly against the gates of Hell under the one blood-stained banner.

In the name of Jesus our Lord we pray.

315

Lord, we pray for the witness of your Church throughout the world. We ask that the distinctive expressions of our various denominations may be welded together in such a way that their unique contributions may strengthen the unity of the whole Church. We pray that worship and witness may be enriched through variety.

Forgive us that we, members of the Church, have concentrated our attention on those things which we think emphasise our uniqueness, and have made them a cause of division among your people. Forgive us, too, that we have been content to promote and present a divided Church to the world. Enhance, we pray, those things that enrich worship and make for effective witness, and give us

courage to abandon those things that hinder the spread of
your truth. For Jesus' and the Kingdom's sake.

316

O God, your Church has been blessed with a variety of
spiritual gifts, and your people endowed with diverse
personalities. Your word has taught us that variety is
intended to strengthen the unity of your people, to guard
them from error, and to make their service more effective.

Throughout the history of the Church, your people have
misused your gifts to pursue personal power, to feed
selfishness and pride, to support stubbornness in face of
correction, or to justify the smug seclusion of denomi-
nationalism. Help us, as your followers, to be sensitive to
our responsibilities in the present age. Save us from any
multiplication of errors, and lead us to a fuller understanding of the unity you desire for your Church.

317

Dear Lord Jesus, during the last days of your earthly life,
you prayed that your disciples would be one, as you and
the Father are one. You also prayed that such unity would
be experienced by all those who came to faith as a result
of the testimony of those first witnesses. We pray for all
those who are actively seeking your will in this matter of
Church unity.

We pray especially for those who hold office in the World
Council of Churches, and all affiliated bodies, as well as
for the individual representatives for various churches.

Give them wisdom and insight in all their deliberations.
We ask this for the sake of your Kingdom.

318

O God, in whom all loving fellowship is found, and in whom all men may meet as brothers, we thank you for the faith that we hold, and for our particular expression of it.

But we ask that by appreciating the witness of fellow believers of other denominations, we might seek to unite in one common witness, so showing to the world that there is unity and a spirit of purpose to be found in Christ.

319

Father, we thank you for your Church on earth. We praise you because your Son Jesus is the head of the Church, and because the Church is his body, empowered by his Spirit and commissioned to do his work and spread his gospel.

We thank you that everyone who acknowledges Jesus as Saviour and Lord is part of the Church, and that each one has been differently gifted by your Holy Spirit in order that Jesus should be glorified, that the fellowship of believers should be strengthened, and that we should serve the world in the name of Jesus Christ.

We pray for the different denominations which make up the one true Church. We praise you that this means your work is done in many different places and that you are worshipped in many different ways. We ask you to forgive us for the fact that far too often we have allowed our denominational differences to become barriers between us, and hinder the preaching of the gospel.

As we seek to work ever more closely with fellow-Christians in various parts of the Church, we ask you to give us spiritual insight so that we can distinguish clearly between those spiritual truths on which we must never compromise, and those things which are merely part of our human tradition.

Father, pour out your Holy Spirit upon the Church so that we might march forward as a mighty army. Give us a holy intolerance of all injustice and oppression. Give us the courage to speak and act for the homeless and the hungry. Give us the wisdom to understand the complex moral issues of our age, and the authority to speak to the world with a prophetic voice. Give us the compassion of Jesus himself so that, with loving hearts and in the spirit of self-sacrifice, we might bring all mankind to know the forgiveness and love of God.

320

Gracious Father, we pray for your holy Christian Church.

Fill it with all truth, and in all truth with all peace.
Where it is corrupt, cleanse it.
Where it is in error, correct it.
Where it is superstitious, rectify it.
Where anything is amiss, reform it.
Where it is right, strengthen and confirm it.
Where it is in want, supply its needs.
Where it is divided and torn apart, heal the divisions,
O Holy One of Israel.

Candidates for the ministry of the gospel

321

Almighty God, when your Son dwelt among us, he chose a handful of men to be his close disciples. In them he rested his confidence for the further proclamation and continuance of the gospel. We thank you for their faithfulness, and for the steadfastness of those who came after, in declaring salvation for the world.

We do not believe, Father, that in our day you will leave yourself without called and chosen ministers of the gospel of redeeming grace. There are those in the world, and perhaps even in this company today, to whom you have spoken and issued a challenge — the challenge to leave home and security, and to follow you.

We pray for those whom you wish to be leaders in the faith, chosen by you and commissioned by the Church. May they hear your voice and respond with joy, knowing that to obey you in the place of your calling is of greater value to the Kingdom than to make sacrifice in the place of their own choosing.

Lord, we pray that you will raise up men and women of spiritual and moral stature, those both older and younger who will be the shepherds of the hungry flock. As they hear and answer the call, grant to them, we pray, gifts of evangelism, of pastoral skills, of management ability, and above all of great love.

We thank you, Lord, for the leaders of our own expression of the Church — those who have been called, chosen, equipped and ordained — and we now bring before you in prayer their successors, both known to us or as yet unknown.

May this genealogy of faith continue through all generations, to the end of the world and to the coming of your Kingdom. In the name of Jesus and for the gospel's sake we pray.

322

Lord Jesus Christ, we praise you for the good news of the Kingdom of God that you brought into the world. We praise you because every day people are hearing that good news, and not only hearing but responding to it. We praise you for the growth of your Church, and especially we praise you for all who have become Christians during the past week. We thank you for all Christians who are fulfilling the responsibility you gave them to proclaim the truth of your Kingdom and who, by their faith, prayer and witness, are helping to make disciples. We pray that your Holy Spirit will continue to equip them and use them.

We know, Lord Jesus, that you require some Christians for specific tasks of leadership in the Church, and we give you thanks today for those spiritual leaders who helped us to grow in our faith. We owe so much to their commitment and their care. We pray for Christian leaders everywhere today, and especially those whom you have called to lead us here in our own fellowship.

We realise the crucial importance of spiritual leadership to the growth of your Kingdom. We remember also that you instructed us to pray for people to serve you in this way. We come now, therefore, to ask that those whom you are calling to this kind of service will discern your will, and be ready and willing to do it.

We make this prayer for the members of our own congregation, and ask that if you are looking for a response from any one of us we shall be quick to say, 'Yes'.

We pray in the power of your name.

323

Today, O God, we bring before you those who sense your call upon their lives, and who are preparing themselves for the ministry of the gospel of Christ.

May they know your presence and guidance as they respond to the glorious challenge placed before them.

Help us to be faithful in prayer for them, and for others in whose lives you are at work, as they make significant choices in their lives.

Father, as we acknowledge that you are Lord, we ask that you will *be* the Lord of all our choices, as we seek, both individually and collectively, to serve and to honour you.

324

Dear God who gives us peace,
Help us to respect our spiritual leaders,
and to be at peace among ourselves.
Use us to encourage the timid and assist the weak;
And to warn and help those who have little energy for you.
May we always be patient
and never pay back wrong for wrong.
Teach us to do good,
and bless us with your wonderful gift of joy.
We know that you want us to be thankful at all times;
May your Spirit always work unhindered in our lives.
Help us to keep what is good
and avoid all that is evil.
Teach us to be faithful to you, as you are faithful to us.
Through Jesus, Our Lord.

(Based on 1 Thessalonians 5:12-24)

325

Father God,
You are holy;
You are special, different, unique, other.
Forgive us when we have failed to acknowledge your holiness,
By warring against life,

By neglecting means of grace,
By being shallow in our worship,
By living lives which do not honour you.

Father God,
We are holy.
We are called out of the world, set apart for special tasks.
Forgive us when we have failed to acknowledge **our** holiness,
By trying to disappear into the crowd,
By living as the world lives,
By denying God-given gifts and talents,
By wasting opportunities to love and serve.

Father God,
You are holy and we are holy.
We have a special relationship with you through your Son.
You have ransomed, healed, restored and forgiven us;
You have cleansed and delivered us from sin;
You have strengthened us to serve you better;
You have given us resurrection life.
Thank you, Father God, in Jesus' name.

326

Dear Lord Jesus, you know the secret sorrows that we each carry; those matters which we are hesitant to share even with our nearest and dearest; those concerns which we lack the words to express; those shadows which lie behind our bright smiles.

At this time, as we pray, Lord, we ask that you will bless:
(With pause after each petition)

That one who is troubled and anxious by a health
　　condition;
That one with financial difficulties;
That one with a problem in the family;
That one who, having given so much to a child that is
　　loved, finds that the child is now so unresponsive
　　and unthoughtful;
That one who carries guilt for words said or unsaid, deeds
　　done or left undone, in the recent or distant past;
That one who awakens in the night, unable to sleep
　　because of depression or worries, whether real or
　　imagined;
That one who cannot come to terms with the loss of a
　　loved one;
That one who feels continued bitterness about a past
　　injustice or unkindness;
That one who is anxious about what the future may hold;
That one who lacks a sense of self-worth.

Lord Jesus, when you walked the dusty roads of Palestine,
you never ignored or passed by those who cried out to
you. As our hearts just now cry out to you, come to each
of us at our point of need with your grace and your
healing.

Give us your eyes and your compassion as we look upon
one another.

Join with us in our concerns, we pray, and give us the
inward assurance that you weep our tears and share our
loads. For your dear name's sake.

327

We look to you, our Father, for every need . . . for you have encouraged us to 'ask and it shall be given you'.

We seek your help for the burdens we carry . . . for you have instructed us to 'seek and you shall find'.

We pray for courage, strength and grace . . . for your word declares: 'Before they call I will answer. While they are yet speaking, I will hear'.

And we give ourselves to loving you, our family and our community . . . 'For God is love, and he that dwells in love dwells in God, and God in him'.

We pray these mercies in your holy name.

At the commencement of a celebration/congress/festival

328

Our Lord, we bow in your presence and honour your name. How we thank you for the happy, vibrant, bonding spirit of our faith.

O Lord, walk with us through these days, these celebration days. Be glorified in us, and let these days be days of blessing, repentance, challenge, commitment, growth.

So much time, energy, prayer and money have been invested in this celebration — and we are ready to celebrate!

We are going to wave our banners and march! We are going to sing songs of praise to Jesus, and clap our hands!

But through all of the celebration, may we hear the heartcry of the penitent! We long to see a packed meeting centre, and we pray for an altar lined with seeking souls!

We anticipate soul-stirring music, heart-gripping drama, spirited preaching, fervent prayer. Speak through the music and song, drama and witness. Speak through our leader, who is your chosen and anointed messenger. Oh, Lord, move in our midst, and lift up your people!

And now, Lord, be pleased to bless our fellowship, in the name of him whom we celebrate we pray.

Index of contributors

Numerical index of prayers and writers

82	GOWANS John	126	CROLY Connie
83	DIXON Grace	127	KEW Clifford
84	CHIN Kathie	128	FAIRCLOUGH Colin
85	ROBSON John	129	SPRIGGS Eileen
86	WOODBURY David	130	GOWANS John
87	HERRON Joy	131	CHASE Marlene
88	FAIRCLOUGH Colin	132	DEVLIN O. Esther
89	WEBBER Howard	133	BANKS Keith
90	WEBBER Howard	134	JAMES Jean
91	WEBBER Howard	135	CARR Irene
92	WEBBER Howard	136	BEGLEY Ian
93	STREET Robert	137	BEGLEY Ian
94	BULL Margaret	138	BEGLEY Ian
95	TONG Joan	139	PHILLIPS Dorothy D.
96	LAWSON Kenneth	140	FAIRCLOUGH Colin
97	LAWSON Kenneth	141	READ Harry
98	LAWSON Kenneth	142	PATERSON Robert
99	PATERSON Robert	143	PATERSON Robert
100	PATERSON Robert	144	PATERSON Robert
101	WHITE Margaret	145	NOYON Hazel
102	REES Marjorie	146	FAIRCLOUGH Colin
103	RYAN Patricia	147	GOWANS John
104	WEBBER Howard	148	VENABLES Marion
105	CAINE Ann D.	149	PHILLIPS Dorothy D.
106	HOSKING Dorothy	150	BANKS Keith
107	HOSKING Dorothy	151	RADER Paul A.
108	REES Marjorie	152	PERRY Geoffrey
109	FAIRCLOUGH Colin	153	CALL Beverly
110	YUILL Chick	154	BARKER David
111	FAIRCLOUGH Tara	155	BARKER David
112	BANKS Keith	156	WHITE Margaret
113	DAVIS Lesa	157	WHITE Margaret
114	ARMISTEAD David	158	REDHEAD Gwenyth
115	BARKER David	159	RYAN Maxwell
116	BARKER David	160	BALE Malcolm
117	BARKER David	161	READ Harry
118	CARR Irene	162	CARR Irene
119	FAIRCLOUGH Colin	163	LAWSON Kenneth
120	CARR Irene	164	LEONARD John
121	JARRETT Elsie	165	HALL L. Cecil
122	FAIRCLOUGH Colin	166	LAWSON Kenneth
123	FRITZ Emily	167	BULL Margaret
124	GAITHER Israel L.	168	STREET Robert
125	SHEPHERD Eleanor	169	BALKHAM David

170	HUNTER Pauline	214	NOYON Hazel
171	FAIRCLOUGH Colin	215	FAIRCLOUGH Colin
172	HUNTER Denis	216	CROLY Connie
173	HUNTER Denis	217	WARD Mabel
174	HUNTER Denis	218	FRITZ Emily
175	HUNTER Denis	219	FRITZ Emily
176	CAMERON A. Faith	220	MARTIN Margaret F.
177	MACLEAN William D.	221	DAVIS Margaret
178	WEBBER Howard	222	SMITH Cleone
179	STACEY Christopher	223	WEBBER Howard
180	BANKS Keith	224	HUNTER Denis
181	LEITCH Eunice	225	HUNTER Denis
182	WOODBURY David	226	TONG Joan
183	GARIEPY Henry	227	GARIEPY Henry
184	FAIRCLOUGH Colin	228	FAIRCLOUGH Colin
185	WEBBER Howard	229	SALVATION ARMY CEREMONIES
186	BEGLEY Ian		
187	BEGLEY Ian	230	SALVATION ARMY CEREMONIES
188	CHASE Marlene		
189	FRITZ Edward	231	FORSTER Edward
190	DAVIS Margaret	232	REES Marjorie
191	LEITCH Eunice	233	WOODBURY David
192	FAIRCLOUGH Colin	234	GARIEPY Henry
193	FAIRCLOUGH Colin	235	THOMPSON Franklyn
194	HUNTER Denis	236	FAIRCLOUGH Colin
195	HUNTER Denis	237	GIRLING Roy
196	HUNTER Denis	238	BEGLEY Ian
197	FORSTER Edward	239	BEGLEY Ian
198	KEN Thomas	240	GIRLING Roy
199	GARIEPY Henry	241	GIRLING Roy
200	FAIRCLOUGH Colin	242	FORSTER Edward
201	WEBBER Howard	243	SALVATION ARMY CEREMONIES
202	WEBBER Howard		
203	COUTTS John	244	DAVIS Margaret
204	MACLEAN William D.	245	HOSKING Dorothy
205	NOYON Hazel	246	DURSTON Rhondda
206	NOYON Hazel	247	GARIEPY Henry
207	HUNTER Denis	248	GARIEPY Henry
208	FAIRCLOUGH Tara	249	FAIRCLOUGH Colin
209	BRYANT Jean	250	BARKER David
210	ABRAMS Ben	251	BARKER David
211	BRUNSON Catherine	252	BARKER David
212	PATERSON Robert	253	HARRIS Wesley
213	PATERSON Robert	254	MORLEY Stephen

255	LUCAS Olive	292	SPRIGGS Eileen
256	DURSTON Graham	293	SMITH Helen
257	STREET Robert	294	WALKER Marie
258	PATERSON Robert	295	PERRY Geoffrey
259	PATERSON Robert	296	ROBSON John
260	DEVLIN O. Esther	297	WOODBURY David
261	DOLLING Kath	298	SMITH Helen
262	HUNTER Denis	299	GARIEPY Henry
263	CHASE Marlene	300	FAIRCLOUGH Colin
264	ROBSON John	301	LEITCH Eunice
265	REDHEAD Gwenyth	302	DURSTON Rhondda
266	NIKOLYCHUCK Marge	303	FAIRCLOUGH Colin
267	MACLEAN William D.	304	WOODBURY David
268	MACLEAN William D.	305	KEW Clifford
269	MACLEAN William D.	306	DURDLE Carson
270	HARRIS Wesley	307	PHILLIPS Dorothy D.
271	HUNTER Denis	308	PHILLIPS Dorothy D.
272	WOODBURY David	309	CROLY Connie
273	GARIEPY Henry	310	RADER Paul A.
274	FAIRCLOUGH Colin	311	THOMPSON Franklyn
275	FAIRCLOUGH Colin	312	GARIEPY Henry
276	FAIRCLOUGH Colin	313	FAIRCLOUGH Colin
277	HUNTER Denis	314	PRATT Will
278	GARIEPY Henry	315	LAWSON Kenneth
279	READ Harry	316	LAWSON Kenneth
280	HUNTER Denis	317	LAWSON Kenneth
281	FRITZ Edward	318	DAWS David
282	ALLEN Ernest J.	319	YUILL Chick
283	GAITHER Israel L.	320	STELSTRA Gerben
284	RYAN Maxwell	321	FAIRCLOUGH Colin
285	KEW Clifford	322	BANKS Keith
286	BALKHAM David	323	SMITH Helen
287	FAIRCLOUGH Colin	324	RYAN Patricia
288	HUNTER Denis	325	PEARCEY Graham
289	FAIRCLOUGH Colin	326	WEBBER Howard
290	STILES Roy	327	FRANCIS William W.
291	DAVIS Lesa	328	MACLEAN William D.